I Am-ness

ISBN: 978-2-9547282-9-2

© 2024 G. Delcourt All rights reserved

Cover Image: Kjpargeter / Freepik

Contact: i.am.ness.pathway@gmail.com

I Am-ness

Pathway to divine Presence

Joseph Delcourt

I Am-ness

FOREWORD[1]

This book is an experience. A channel, a baton passed in the flow of our lives. Its intent is neither to stimulate our imagination or thoughts, nor to teach, even less to distract ourselves. It is just about remembering.

See this little book as a box in an attic, where long forgotten memories have been stored or concealed, to be eventually re-discovered. You are about to bring them in the open again and this is a moment of true joy.

Or it could be just as well a poetic wandering within wonders, to be listened to without the need to understand, begetting minute moves motioned by an active song that whispers within ourselves.

---

[1] In the following pages, the 1,2, 3... numbers refer to footnotes which complement, document or broaden the text. The i,ii,iii... letters refer to endnotes with bibliographical information.

It tells a **reality that precedes all that we may experience**, which, deep, deep within us, we already know. At the end of this journey into awareness, what we took for granted will only remain as a faltering echo of our experiences, our interrogations and inspirations.

Each of us is on his way, on her path, some take it easy, others soldier on, many make long detours. There is no hurry in the infinite perspective of life. In Reality, all is exactly in place. Everything is just a journey within perfection. We all try and travel our lives as well as we can, with our backpacks, whether heavy or light, filled with the tools, props and belongings which are our own: what we were born with, remnants of our encounters, explorations and roams, our acts, thoughts, intents, and the awareness that nurture them.
And love above all, under whichever form.

Our lives are those long and winding roads within what *IS* which we resist so much, and what follows is an invitation to peek into this overwhelming landscape. A wonderful, extraordinary voyage between what we believe and what we are, between what moves us and what names us, between what we choose and what precedes us. A journey within, towards a Reality which is truly ours, which we all share, and struggle so much to perceive as it is. At the end of the day, being alive may simply mean accepting to be transformed. To become.

But first, a word of caution: because of its very nature, this book is imperfect, uncomplete, certainly inaccurate in many respects. It is a mere sketchy, furtive glance into what *Is*. It is unfinished, and anyone who feels inspired to may push the experience forward. It is riddled with silences and absences, which are more meaningful than all the many words it contains.

These pages tell no truth nor attempt to ascertain any. Truth is but a multifaceted, changing, temporal whim. What was true yesterday will no longer be tomorrow. Or later, another day. Each of us simply has his or her own that has been built along what he discovered, what she suffered, enjoyed and lived.

Truth is what lays beyond us, immeasurable and it does not belong to us.

Conversely, it is fitting to say that what this book has in offering is a measly image of Reality. As we already know or will discover soon enough, Reality evades any attempt to be put into words and forms, in phrases and thoughts.

The Dao that can be spoken is not the eternal Dao
The name that can be named is not the eternal
name[i]

In this journey, do not let the words stop you, do not believe what they say, just try and feel that which they contain and cannot be described. Let yourself be touched by the unspeakable.
The wisest, the most necessary perhaps, would be not to mull too much over this book and read it as a tale, and whenever a word or a phrase arrests you, stop by for a while, as if at a hostel at the stage: to have a little rest but not stay long

Our hearts and intellects are of this world, they are not the appropriate vehicles for a journey to the Source. They cannot even near it from eons away. The Source is and touches in the brevity and intensity of lightning. Suddenly, It passes through us, opens and transforms us, leaves a trace there and we do not exactly know whence and since when. The Source is this *presence* within, that is silent and tranquil, a scent so delicate and powerful that there is nothing to do but stay quietly put, listen, be filled and let oneself be acted upon.

Marvel.

Beyond the words, let this book resonate with your own sense of being, this feeling that foreshadows consciousness, the faint remembrance of something that is about to happen, a **meaningful blank** like an amnesiac's memory. *"There is something there, but I can't exactly say what."*

There is something is this absence, there is a sound in this silence, there is presence in this darkness.

That's all there is.

I Am-ness

PREAMBLE

I Am-ness

Ultreia! [ii]

As we engage further into this reading, we may unnoticingly have taken tiny steps towards the immense, still and silent *I* we all carry.
The *I* that is at peace whatever happens.

Make yourself comfortable and welcome what follows as a stroll that will take you into a landscape that you live in, which you are more or less at home with but will undoubtedly recognise.
Exactly as if you were wandering into a place the habits of which you are not yet quite familiar with. Not a foreign one, nothing is foreign in what follows. All along the path, you will discover or recall, get weary or happy, patient or impatient. You wonder. What matters is to engage and keep walking because, in the long run, one gets used to it and the path gets made.
And if you have already started your journey within, you will indeed find all along these pages, traces of your own voyage. Undoubtedly, each experience is unique, and we will, on many an occasion, perceive things differently. This is one of this world realities: any being is a fragment of the very same kaleidoscope, diversity is part of reality.

Just like in the story of the blind men and the elephant.

Let the energy take shape and the evidence grow within, fragile and persistent all at once. Fragile because it is faint and unprovable, persistent because it keeps knocking at our doors, whispering *"keep on going!"*. Like a signal that is imperious and gentle at the same time. A powerful experience that is nothing of the certain though, something like the fragrance of recognition and gratitude. A sudden *"but of course"* that awakes a causeless joy.
If you rejoice at what precedes, beautiful will be the moments to come.

It may just as well happen that, here, you tell yourself that clearly this book is not for you. Just drop it, forget it, it may come back later in your life. Or not. This is of no importance whatsoever. And if ever you engage in this passage, you know as well that you can take a bit of a distance at any time and resume the reading whenever you feel inclined to.

The story begins

One thing is for sure, this story takes us on the path of pure wonder. No other state is possible, it surpasses them all.

Very gradually we are given the ability to sense, to let a feeling of the great mystery grow within. Of That which *is* this world and not *of* this world. Something like in the A. Hitchcock's movie *"Rear window"*: somehow distractedly at first and then with more attention, you observe from the distance a scene that is none of your business. You do not exactly understand what is going on, but you get interested. You catch bits and pieces which you keep stitching together until something appears that seems to hold up. And that makes this little book.

This is precisely when you inescapably hear footsteps in the corridor and the one you were observing and trying to figure out, comes knocking at your door.

Tada!

Yes, this story holds up just enough for you to get going because, at the end of the day, it is your *I* which you are going to. The one who knocks at your door is none other than your *I*. A *I* that has grown, luminous, unrecognizable and who knows so much.

Now is the time to talk about the creation of the world.

Just That.

That is where we go.
Can you feel a tremor inside, a feverish anticipation of what may come next? Like a joy that dares not believe it.
...
Well, what about this story then?

"Once upon a time". This too is rather fitting. One could even say *"A time only once"*: once is, has been and will ever be enough. In this story, there is no beginning nor end as, in all likelihood, we are living a *present* in all eternity.
We live the big *"happily ever now"*.

Let us begin.

There is...Nil.

Yes, you read well, there is Nil. Nil not as in nothing, not in the negative form because there is no negation in this state. This is a Nil-state, with no opposition of any sort. Nil in all times, in all eternity.

Nought.

A rather knowledgeable person asked once the question *"why is there something rather than nothing?"* [iii]

One must say, to begin with, that the fact that something exists *is* the absolute miracle. The life's, Creation's accuracy goes far beyond any possible understanding whilst we can witness it daily when, by chance, contemplation or profession, we peek into the order of things: the meticulous equilibrium between the forces that hold matter, planets, stars and galaxies.
These forces that govern the organisation of our cells, their minute adjustment to the functions that are theirs, their so precise collaboration. Not forgetting how fitting were the conditions that led

to the coming of life on our planet in the first place[1].

If it had happened by chance, its probability would be between 10^{-30} and 10^{-36}, that is one preceded by 30 to 36 zeros after decimal point! Which player would ever gamble with such a probability[2]?

Yet.

When we ask ourselves why all is, if we let our consciousness drift beyond thoughts, if we allow a sort of subtle fragrance to infuse within, something starts taking shape: we may sense a surge of premonitory exhilaration merged with some sort

---

[1] « *The universe was very precisely created for the emergence of life and consciousness. The initial setting could be compared to the mastery of an archer who can hit with his arrow in the midst of a target that is 1 centimetre wide and 15 billion light-years afar*» Trinh Xuan Thuan.

[2] The multiverse theory states that this is no probability: our universe would just be one among an *infinity* of universes, the one endowed with such proper "life" conditions. But this is just pushing the question a bit further: how did this multiverse come to existence and what would other forms of life be then?

of a panic. The hunch of awe in enormous proportions.

The nameless is the origin of Heaven and Earth
The named is the mother of myriad things
Thus, constantly without desire, one observes its essence
Constantly with desire, one observes its manifestations
These two emerge together but differ in name
The unity is said to be the mystery
Mystery of mysteries, the door to all wonders.[iv]

Now comes the ultimate ginormous.
What there is in the immeasurable nature of Nil is only the possibility, the intent of something.
The only possibility that can be in Nil is the **Intent to Be.** None else. Can we really get that in earnest?

The Intent to Be.

It is utterly impossible, one had better not try, to get even the slightest idea of the unconceivable power of the *Intent to Be* within Nil.

The *Intent to Be*, nothing else. In Nil.

Are we truly able to have a sense of this unthinkable tension, this eternal, silent and vibrant

19

equilibrium between Nil and the Intent of All? **This Intent is essential, crucial because it prompts All that will come next.**

A Being in intent (in-tension), an indescribable tension between two primordial impulses that are mutually bound: the *Yang* impulse which creates, engenders, expresses, the energy of expansion which combines with the *Yin* impulse that contains and restrains, the energy of form, of nourishment, of structure and limitation.

Are we able to let ourselves be pervaded by this unthinkable tension that spirals to the infinite, between that which propels and that which retains, between the impetus and its opposite, between the surge and the limit, do we feel the sheer power of this potential energy that is preliminary to Creation?[1]

In this unspeakable tension, there is not even "*I am*" awareness, as this is nil.

---

[1] If you have ever engaged into an endeavour out of nothing, you surely have felt this urge to act (filled with interrogation) together with the need to give it shape and form, to define limits (filled with reassurance). This is exactly what it is about, scale apart of course!

What may come out of this In-tension in equilibrium in nothingness, can only be all there is. The unconceivable potential of the totality of all. All in nil, all in coming, all in intent out of nothing. This is neither an opposition nor a substitute, this is a completeness rather, an unwavering tension, an eternal and perfect equilibrium in the absolute, a tautology[1] beyond any proportion.

The *profoundness* of the Dao.

Everything is in place and will repeat at every level of Creation, whether perceivable to our senses or not. This mindboggling embrace of two impulses that are mutually bound, designs the *Intent to be*[2]. These are the two impulses at the origin of Creation [v]. This is a Reality that precedes us, comprehends us, overwhelms us, utterly unthinkable.

Just to think about that really does something!

No created being may ever get the slightest glimpse of the immeasurable power of the *Intent to Be* in nil. It is totally beyond any awareness level

---

[1] A proposition that is true whatever the perspective you consider it from.

[2] The *Khadir Ilham* (Islam)

of Creation, even more so our ability to apprehend, we humans as we are.

Speaking of a story, is not this one absolutely staggering?

In our attempts to name this unspeakable, unreachable Reality, some use the words God[1], Brahma, Allah[2], YHWH[3], the Dao. All these names, so diverse, which we give It, only speak of our differences and separations.

Others do not give It a name, and so much the better: avoid naming It if you can. A name confers a finite dimension, a form to what has none. It almost sounds like a summon, a demand to believe

---

[1] « *The one who hears the word God does not perceive Real but an illusion, an image of Real. It goes the same with the words Father, Son, Holy Ghost, Life, Light, Resurrection, Church and all the rest. These words do not speak of Reality. We will understand when we experience Real. All the words we hear in this world can only deceive us* » Gospel of Philip (plate 101-11).

[2] Allah is neither God's name nor one of God's names. It is only a description (*the One who enfolds*)

[3] "*I Am Who I Am*". The Letters are not supposed to be spoken. Instead, *HaVaYaH* is pronounced.

and not search. An end. Well, you must search however, set yourself in motion, explore, inquire. Coining a wonderful Taoist phrase, *Wei Wu Wei* (act and act not), one must search and search not.

Here, we call It the Source.

All of the sudden[1], the equilibrium is broken: At its climax, the *Intent to Be* gets aware of itself, the *Intent to Be* becomes *Sense of Being*. Intent that is infinitely potent and Sense that contains it infinitely[2].

Here is the "*I Am*" Awareness. *I Am-ness*.

Now *IS* a state of Awareness, a pure spirit, prior to any thought, any intelligence, as opposed to *consciousness* that is the work of mind, the manipulation of concepts with the support of thoughts.

A primordial "*I Am*" far beyond the confines of all knowledge[3]. The *Am* breeds the *I*. A *I* that is

---

[1] In a manner of speaking, as time does not exist *at that point*.

[2] *HaVaYaH* and *Elokim*

[3] « *Any consciousness of being, any manifestation of 'I'ness, derives from this primordial I which echoes within any created*

consequent and not precedent to the state of being.

And this Intent manifests as *Light*.

In order to allow that very state of *I Am-ness* to pervade us, we must let go of any reference to self, of this reflex movement of thought towards oneself. There is no *I*, only *Be* in its fullness. A verb and no subject.

By the way, for what purpose does *I Am-ness* arise?

Out of your own profoundness, you can find only one 'reason' for this to happen: **the unspeakable, unstoppable power of Love**. Love as an intent and love as a state all at once. Only for love does one come out the equilibrium of oneself. Love ultimately is what propels us out of our comfortable selves. Actually, and we will witness that all along this book, LOVE IS ALL WHAT IS, Love is *Presence* at its utmost.
Love is the reason why all is. There only is Love, the totality of the Universe is made of Love. One exists,

---

being or thing. Initially and ultimately only God is I » Terence Gray (Wei Wu Wei) in 'Fingers pointing towards the moon'.

gets born and creates only from love, nothing else whatever the form it may take.

As Love will accompany us all along this story, let us consider it a bit further.

Love to that extend is impossible to tell. Love not of the other, not of oneself, not of what is or what could be, not of anyone or anything. Love solely as a pure state, a state in bliss, an irresistible impulse and an absolute fulfilment all at once, which creates and embraces the world it will become.

Infinitely, eternally.

Love that is unconceivable and all-powerful[1]. Love that creates and carries each and everything. Instantly.

"Love is nothing without Light
Light is nothing without Love"[vi]

So as to get a feeble sense of this Reality, try and imagine a dot, as tiny as possible and be carried by

---

[1] Cf this text written between 1296 and 1306 by a beguine burnt at the stake as heretic *"I am God, says Love, as Love is God and God is Love and this (liberated) soul is God by the condition of Love"* (The Mirror of simple and wiped-out souls – Marguerite Porete).

its minuteness, feel the **unconceivable energy** it contains.

.

Consider the dot hereabove, hovering as if detached from the page, let it fill your inner space with its presence and all that it contains. You may feel something silently vibrant which is not void and from which you cannot detach yourself. This is truly phenomenal. The Source, the absolute *One-Presence* is utterly punctual, it knows no space nor time. It is.

Initial and final point.

The Source speaks to us with instantaneous and silent lightning speed, intuitive flashes far beyond light-speed that ignore the slow and laborious work of our neurons and of our intellect. Awareness far beyond knowledge.

Love *at this point* is incandescence for any being of matter that tries to near it, what mystics of all times have told, chanted and heralded with so much persistence.

Love *at this point* brings tears to our eyes and laughter to our mouth all at once, so much our hearts are overwhelmed by confusion when we draw near to it, so much it is impossible to contain. Whatever we are given to experience and feel in the realm of love on this Earth is merely an echo, a minuscule wavelet on a beach that tells the unsounded storm out there, in the open sea.

Now (!) there *IS* something: '*I Am-ness* emerges out of naught, all at once in full awareness of Itself and bearer of the lightning strike of the primal *Intent to Be*.

Instantly, Creation is. Every universe of all times and spaces. All at once. All species, all stories, all senses of being, all meanders of life, bound to evolve through time towards ultimate *I Am-ness*.

Out of the primal and stable tension in nil, something has come into being. One[1] gets born out of zero. All is, because **there can only be ALL in the primeval Oneness**. Creation in its wholeness. Creation as a quantic song of all possibilities.
Creation/'*I am*', eternal and infinite, brought about by the continuous entanglement of the two primeval principles, the twin impulses *Yang/Intent*

---

[1] One is often seen as the first number. It is the last as well, the one that contains them all.

to be and *Yin/Sense of Being*, which eternally combine.

Since All is, our own world too comes into being, the universe that is perceptible to our senses and conceivable with our thoughts, sprouted up from this very moment, together with all the others that are not[1]. This is the *Big Bang* as we conceive it, a space-time continuum, as creation appears to us. It would be fitting to name it a *Prodigious Bang* rather, as ALL is simultaneously created, including what has no tangible form, what is out of space-time which, like the immerged part of the iceberg, is far greater and deeper than the emerged one.

All is, inhabited by ultimate *I Am-ness,* which is common to all that which exists. **Nothing created, with or without form, is devoid of *'I am' ness,*** including anything at the matter level, which is the most basic *Presence* plane.
At whichever realm of Creation, *Presence* lays, the awareness of being.

Without *Presence*, there is *Nil*.

---

[1] A rather good image of where our perceptible world stands within creation could be the electro-magnetic spectrum, which seamlessly spans from zero to infinite.

Presence is really all there is, all that can be. All is Awareness (*Presence*) and *Presence* is the vibration of Love. Creation in its entirety, whether perceptible or not, is an infinite array of awareness fields, an unconceivable soundboard that expresses all the possibilities of being, from the utterly coarse to the ultimately refined.

Life and *presence* are but the same reality, seen from two different angles (biological/symbolical, physical/metaphysical, experiential/conceptual...). Life, Creation, *presence,* love are but one single reality.

Again, another tautology. Everything in this story is truly overwhelming.

"All that is part of our visible world manifests a given state of awareness. Every form that is visible from the outer is the expression an inner awareness" [vii]

Our perceptible world is a very limited slice of the Creation infinite, that is specific to our awareness field[1], and so much the better as it prevents us

---

[1] And it works both ways: when your awareness grows, so evolves your perception of the world.

from losing our minds[1]. Thus, in our world, *I Am-ness* appears to our senses by an illusion of separateness purposely created by our senses and our intellect. They are precisely made for this: for creating separations among beings and things to make it possible for us to "play" (work and act), to experience *Love* within the awareness fields that are accessible to us. These are vast and but relatively crude ones, just a tiny part of Reality.

Creation is *One-ness* (one-awareness) that vibrates in constant exchanges between an infinity of frequency degrees. A gigantic soundless music. This, in turn, is also true for our manifested world: *"the universe is a participatory universe [2]"*. What we perceive of it derives from what we are.

---

[1] Our world is like a swimming pool where we safely learn how to swim before diving into the wider ocean.

[2] John Wheeler. Cf. " *the content of consciousness is the ultimate reality, and it is not possible to coherently formulate the laws of quantum mechanics without referring to consciousness"* (Eugène Wigner, Nobel Prize for physics) - *"I cannot imagine a theory of all that is coherent while ignoring consciousness"* (Andrei Linde – one of the developers of the theory of the universe inflation).

I Am-ness: there cannot be anything else, there actually is nothing else and this is of breathtaking beauty.

Here, we must speak of Descartes. What we chose to keep from his writings takes the matter from the wrong end, the one that creates distance instead of bringing closer. Cartesians express the truth of creative *Presence* backwards: *"cogito ergo sum".* I think therefore I am. Reality is precisely the other way round: *"sum ergo cogito".* **I am, before anything else, then I think.** One could even say *sum ergo... all the rest.*

I am, this is why I think. Naturally. Thinking as an expression of *I Am-ness*, but not the only one.

Do not you feel this is so much more beautiful and powerful?
Can you sense how it clears us from the cages of thought and intellectualism, how suddenly our spirit begins to fly, all awareness freed, to heights and summits that were denied to it?

The all-Presence of I Am-ness.

Back to the *Big Bang:* for all of us, it is this infinitesimal and pivotal instant when *I Am-ness* gets born out of its equilibrium within Nil. This truly miraculous and sublime moment when the All comes out of nought.

Now surges the unconceivable inflation of the universe in our world made of time and space.

At this stage, our world is but an *"ocean of light"*[1] when it is "all" in the making. A unified field, a primordial and opaque soup which expanses billions of times within a flash of lighting, becomes transparent and fragments into quarks, protons, neutrons, atoms, eventually giving birth to trillions and quadrillions of stars, galaxies, planets, molecules and living beings. The chronological story of our manifested world is born.

The utter beauty and power of what this is about are unspeakable.

These simultaneous inflation and fragmentation are the exact and perceptible manifestations of the two primordial impulses that are at the origin of Creation: the creative impulse of conception-

---

[1] An unconceivable emission of photons created by the continuous annihilation of **mater-anti mater particle couples generated by the energy of vacuum** (!). Moved by the two primordial impulses, these exactly and continuously oppose each other. Only a little proto matter subsided from this utter chaos which gave birth to our universe.

expansion-activity and the creative impulse of form-limitation-**attraction/repulsion**.

These two mutually intricated impulses inseparably express the Source, the Origin, each with its own purpose, and their continuous embrace takes multiple forms; it notably expresses within our world as the electro-magnetic radiation.

"LIGHT is similar to light. Only the intensity differs."viii

What we are, our individual beings (our soul, inner self) and our ego (our conscious/subconscious self), result too from these two impulses: the intent to be/grow intertwined with attraction-repulsion/separateness. The perception of a separated "I" is inherent to the creation of the world. It is the **necessary illusion** that enables us to experience the *All-Presence* under its every possible forms.

Here we stand at the heart of the *optical illusion of consciousness* coined by A. Einstein[1].

---

[1] *"A human being is a part of a whole which we name Universe. A limited part in time and space. He experiences himself, his thoughts and emotions, as separated from the*

33

The illusion of separateness enables the *One-Presence* to experience Being in its absolute entirety and diversity. One must get out of oneself to experience multitude, which is irrevocably endless.
It cannot be otherwise.

No individuation would mean no Creation, hence no experience of *All-I Am-ness*.

Now, you may sense how the *One-Awareness* dilutes itself, dissolves but does not disappear into every *presence* field of Creation, from unthinkable heights of embrace down to the ones we are able to perceive via our senses or conceive within our minds, which form our manifested world.

The equilibrium *within* the Source, **the Intent to Be within Nil**, remains in all eternity, entirely inaccessible, since reaching it would be losing form and any sense of being[1]. And at the same time (!)

---

rest, a kind of optical illusion of consciousness" (A. Einstein's letter 1950).

[1] « *The Lord said, thou shalt not be able to see my face; for man cannot see me and live.* » (Exodus)

the Source is **All-Presence**, entirely contained and disseminated within the whole Creation.

Nil and All at the same time.
There we are.

Henceforth, the feel grows of what purpose Creation may carry: **to share a prodigious *Sense of Being***, a reciprocal, instantaneous and eternal exchange between the Source's *Intent to be* **and** Creation which manifests It (*Sense of Being*).

An unconceivable conversation between *Intent to Be* and *Sense of Being*.
At every level.

A marvel.

In fact, we are continuously living this exchange within our sensitive world: as soon as we perceive, watch, listen, taste, touch, smell, see, as soon as we radiate an intent, conceive a thought, complete an act, achieve a project... we all at once **act in consciousness** (a brain activity within this world) **and enact awareness** (*Intent to Be* and *Sense of Being* which participate in eternity). Similarly, when we interact with other beings, animals, plants or things.

We constantly exchange with/within the *One-Presence.*

For the very simple reason that this silent and forever active *Presence* that is at the origin of all, dwells at the deepest or us, within the vacuum within our electrons and protons, at the heart of every atom.

From it, we borrow our own **sense of being**.

All forms, whether physical, mental, emotional, are awareness vibrations, variations within the *One I Am-ness.* Like the waves on the ocean: some are dreadfully gigantic, others absolutely minute, but each is an expression of the ocean might.

And if you want to try and have a feel of the magnitude of this, consider it all happens instantaneously, punctually, not in a successive manner, as time and space only exist in our world.

You may experiment this, here and now: try and be aware of your sight together with your intent to see when you look, of your hearing together with your intent to hear when you listen, of your sensation when you touch, of your taste when you savour, of your sense when you smell. Put yourself in this state when you take consciousness of you alive. Then you may have a flavour of your being at the deepest of who you are.

There you get a tiny bit closer to your *presence,* that is just an instant in the *One-Presence.* A wavelet.

Did you notice? Joy is there.

Now, let us have a little geometric digression, an experiment that you can do in your turn if you deem it useful. All you need is a compass, a ruler, a set square and a pencil. Draw a circle inside another circle twice its size. It touches both the centre and the circumference of the bigger circle. You should get something that looks like initiating the Yin-Yang symbol of the Dao. If you make the small circle roll but not slide inside the big one, each point on its circumference draws a straight line. So, **two opposite points draw a *cross*.** This shows the perfect balance of the Dao, the Yin and Yang in absolute equilibrium within itself, Creation in gestation. The two contradictory impulses united in an endless embrace. The cross is a description of the gigantic dynamics within the point.

This may explain why the first crosses, the Celtic, Druidic, Mayan ones were all inscribed in a circle.

Now, for the same reason as the one mentioned above, the small circle comes out of the big one, the balance is broken. *"I Am-ness"* and creation appears. Proceed likewise, put the same small circle outside the large one and observe what a point on its circumference describes as it rolls around the large one. Each point now draws the shape of a petal and if you carry on with the experiment, level after level, there appears the image of a **gigantic rose with no limit and no end**[1]. A rose in the unthinkable and beautiful multitude of its petals.

---

[1] The *Aum* mandala of Buddhists is probably the same rendering. So were the cathedrals *rosettes*.

The *cross* and the *rose*.

The *inner* as a stable and balanced tension between two perfectly contradictory impulses, the *outer* as their glorious and unthinkable manifestation.

This geometry, these symbols tell the whole Creation out of nil. Creation in-tention then in Reality. From zero one is born, then two, three and all the rest. Instantaneously. Zero and Infinity. There we are and there we are going back. All and nil.

From then on (!), things get organised, the whole universe, all universes are created. The ones we see, those we do not and those we have no clue about. All is, in all eternity.

This is the whole story. Creation within naught. It is impossible to figure out and it leaves us stunned. To the point where we feel a sort of frozen joy, a joy we dare not believe, so close we are to marvel. This is the story which will guide us on our way, our compass. This is the Path that men and women of *Spirit* of all times have taken, by which they have been inspired and illuminated. A journey back to the Source of Creation, like tireless fish which, without respite, swim up endless rivers to the point where they were born.

This is the star to which anchor our voyage so as not to get lost on our way.

I Am-ness

THE INTENT TO BE

I Am-ness

A path

Where do we go?

That is simple, we are treading homewards. This path leads us Home. Home to the deepest of what we are and that dwells within, to the most complete and most real experience of being alive. We are treading a path that takes us to the **unmeasurable magnificent Reality, that we carry and which we are.**

This *home* is us, our being which we may have forgotten, littered with all that stirs us apart. A Home in immortal *Presence*, which makes the world most beautiful because unified, detached from any veil of ego and separateness.

In three words as in a hundred, **we are apprentices**: we are being taught how to go beyond what we think we are, beyond our agitation within the story of ourselves, willed and sustained by our ego, to reach to the full reality of our sense of being.

Moving from the story into Reality.

On this way to detachment, that is to the opening to "larger [1]" awareness fields, we may at times be given a few understandings, enlightening and lasting insights. Here, to comprehend is more to resonate than to reason. To be aspired as if magnetised into another *presence* plane that is wider and deeper. A superior plenitude. Above all, not the result of any intelligence process. Quite the opposite actually: an awareness comes to us, immediate and like a lightning strike, which can even catch us unprepared.

Each of us is a prodigious pile of experiences and lives. In each experience and life, we may choose to experience a single *presence* plane, the one we were born in. We may choose to be what we have been from birth, to get caught in a story that spans over multiple generations. We may just as well choose to explore, to venture into other fields, to broaden our sense of being to vaster and more complete horizons. Or, by choice, error, lapse or folly, drift down into cruder or more limited planes.

---

[1] Not in a hierarchical sense but of a progressive inclusion, exactly as with the matryoshkas.

To be is to be inhabited by *presence* and roam within it all at once.

At the end of the day, there no better nor worse choice to make, all is in its place. All choices, all experiences are effective, each one is a journey within Reality. The only question is which awareness plane do we choose to actuate in our experience of life and of how long we will remain apprentices.

As soon as we understand that living is about experiencing an awareness field, we may choose to remain there or change. Most of the time, it goes by itself: when our being is sated with an experience it has lived to the fullest, it naturally moves on. Something else comes to it, something happens.

There you may have a hint of the astoundingly perfect game between awareness planes, intents, perceptions, acts and realities. You have a glimpse of the world you live in, of your place within it, of the experiences that come to you and, most important of all, how you may *realise* what you are. In every sense of it.

Every life event, every circumstance is an opportunity for *raising awareness:* each of them is a proposal to transform and broaden, to evolve in awareness. Which you catch or not.

Most of the time, this process that takes place in the depth of your sense of being goes unnoticeable. That is how it should be because what happens outside of the ego is usually not perceived by the heart or the intellect. You simply realise, one day, that you have changed.

Whatever you may feel or think about this, just try and stay in peace as much as you can. A tiny puff of wind may be seen at the surface of calm waters but goes unnoticed in an agitated sea.

There is no point in wanting to move fast, in rushing the movement. Just be attentive to the *"ah, but of course!"* moment. Should it come, it signals that you have let yourself be approached, you resonated with That which is within each of us. Without the need to put it in words, you caught a glimpse of the *I* dimension you carry and that is You. This *I*, that is gigantic, discreet and vertiginous.

To be home is nowhere else than where you are.

Never.

At the end of the day, we go nowhere else than where we are, in a distanceless and timeless voyage, a transformation that is motionless and unnoticeable. You surely do not have to be anyone else than who you are, which is reassuring rather.

There is no more beautiful journey than to go and find out who we really are, to discover That which dwells within, the source of all joys, all marvels.

It is all about re-discovering that we are.

This is not a point of effort, of virtue nor deprivation. Nor of hope. No, nothing of the sort. Hope, search for virtue or effort drive us out of ourselves, strengthen our egos, make us believe there is something out there to be reached or achieved, somewhere outside of ourselves, while actually all there is, is therein.

To be.
Simply
In presence.

There you will understand all that you have lived.

All these human lives have a very simple reason for being: **we, humans, are learning how to live in awareness.**

Yes, reread these words: to learn how to live in awareness, that means being aware of what one thinks, says, does **and** to live oneself as well as experiencing oneself as a chunk of awareness, all at once.

To be *present*.

This journey is no promise of an easier life. This may happen as a consequence though, but this is not the intention for it. When you walk long-distance, you tread along highs and lows, and you know that you cannot side-step any. You accept them all and you walk in peace.

What this is about is a life that is more complete, more present and certainly tastier, where everything you are meant to be takes on a particular flavour, a surprise as much as something you already know.

A present of some sort.

Here, you may tell yourself *"One may very well enjoy life and live it well without bothering about all those things"*. You are perfectly right. Enjoying life is in the order of things too; pondering about it is in no way the assurance of avoiding the highs and lows that come to us, our little misfortunes and the big ones, the worries, the pains, and the joys.

On the contrary. As we speak of the All, it necessarily implies that what "good" or "bad" comes to us, what fills or empties us, what makes us grow or dwindle must be seen in the same light, with the same acceptance. We must try and forget about our preferences.
Ah! here comes another story.

Just for a moment, imagine we are fish.

We wander as we please in an ocean that is so vast and immeasurable that it looks limitless, so much so that none of us have travelled to its boundaries. It extends into mysterious depths that keep unsounded and obscure. There, most of us live rather well (or nearly) in a liquid universe, immense and loaded with mysteries, that we try to make our own and elucidate. Therein, every species cohabits and strives to survive as well as it can. There are the powerful and the destitute, the greedy, the small, the gregarious and the lonely, the swift and the slow, those who play and those who hunt, those who swim in depths and those who come close to the surface.

One day, one of the latter, then two, a hundred and eventually a whole species gets to open air, discovers air, wind and light. A completely new world of which they knew merely nothing. Of course, there have been these glittering shimmers under the surface, waters that felt warmer, bubbles that disappeared into the surface and artefacts that fell out of nowhere. Of course.

However, the quasi-certainty of this world next door never prevented the vast majority of fish to keep on living joyfully in their usual world, to the point that it has never been questioned whether this is the only one that exists. Scorpion fish and red mullet frolic in the rocks, clown fish play with the anemones and marvel at their colours in the coral reefs, schools of herring dance and race, rays fly imperial and graceful while others, the explorers mentioned above, insistently keep on with their discovery. They even get used to this adjacent world, they cosy up into it, so to speak, they learn how to breathe, to be more at ease, and they start to evolve. So much so that, one day, they turn batrachians and change nature. To the point that, one day, they disappear from the oceans, they change form and live elsewhere a totally different life, keeping the memory of the time when they were fish. Some return under the surface, as penguins, frogs or seals do. Other, like dolphins, whales or flying fish prefer to make a few brief playful forays into the open, taste its flavour, allow themselves to marvel at it for a while and then return to their liquid world. Others, lastly, resolutely turn to this new life.

Become humans.

Here is where we have to come to, here is the direction for this path: to be able to get out of our ocean, in our turn become batrachians of some sort and, if possible, go further. To be able, now that we know of this other world, to have the courage, patience and tenacious tranquillity to direct our steps to it, three qualities that are indispensable for the wanderers we are.

There we go.

We set out to this luminous, subtle and airy world that covers, surrounds and mingles with ours, so intricate that we are unaware of it: the realm of the Real or realised Human, coined by others as the Anthropos, heaven or the Kingdom. This *presence* state which simply is our destiny, what we are called to be.

Now is probably the right moment for you to get your going if you have not already. Leave right away, leave as you are, do not even take the time to change, it will happen soon enough on the way.

Everyone trudges on his or her own transformation path. Whether he/she wants to or not. Each of us lives as she/he pleases or can and all together we make a delicious mix. All is beautiful, all is legitimate, all is courageous, and we can only share our experiences and perspectives with love and with respect.

All similar, each particular.

On this path towards one-self, no knowledge is required, no cultural, religious or intellectual baggage is needed. While you are at it, try and keep it as light as possible, with as little creed or conviction as possible. This path requires neither preparation or accessory, nor practice or complicated exercise. Only a gentle and tranquil complicity with silence perhaps, plus two or three additional qualities that you will discover on your way.

How do you know you are on the right path?

Oh, this is rather simple: firstly, one **never knows for sure**. This would be both sheltering and fallacious. To set off is to put your confidence at test. There will undoubtedly be moments in the plenty when you walk without a sign, without a mark, without anybody to provide you with comfort, reassurance or conversation. You make a step forward without knowing what on, you move forward blindly, you trudge and struggle, you even get lost and suddenly rejoice when on a milestone, a tree or at the corner of a house, appears a little indication. Or when someone who stopped by at the side of the road tells you that she too is on her way. Then you stop in your turn, have a little chat and rest until you get started again for a little way together.

Anyway, certainties are dangerous, and experience shows that they, more than anything else, are what causes our misguidance. All of them. It is better to walk in uncertainty, in question rather than in affirmation.

Hence, you confide without being sure and this is what makes confidence beautiful. Comes progressively a peaceful and natural joy, something true and unforced. You feel home while on your way. You feel that, at the end of the day, you risk nothing, and that fearfulness is useless. From then on, the universe around gets quieter, circumstances and people get congenial, amicable, smile a bit more. Life takes a flavour of peaceful interrogation that is neither fear nor expectancy. Like a child happy to discover rather.

Next, and this is more difficult to get on with, **there is nowhere to arrive.**
Nowhere. This is the unspeakable beauty of Creation. A way of *presence* is a path with no end. We might as well accept it right away because *that* is what gives the instant all its weight (Now-here).[1]

Sailors know that: the horizon is no destination. The profound reality of Creation is infinite. Not that it is unfinished, it is but its very nature is infinity (seen from the perspective of space) and eternity (seen from the perspective of time). This

---

[1] Like in the story of the two zen Buddhist monks walking their long way to the monastery: after a long taxing while, the youngest asks « When will we arrive, Master ? ». The elder replies « Here we are ».

is a truth we had better not to try and comprehend but accept. Our intellect, our intelligence which is made for this finite world is not able to grasp eternity. This is an unreachable notion, just like the horizon above, a truth which cannot be approached, that evades when we get closer.

The only possibility when we stroll towards the horizon is to rejoice for every moment; for each and every of them. For encounters, circumstances, joys and efforts, moments that are easy or difficult.

Here and now. Always.

This is how we humans get a whiff of eternity.

This reality may be read the other way round: each time you feel you have arrived somewhere, when you think you have understood something, you had better get cautious and know this is at best a temporary truth, a decoy at worst. Do not nestle on it too long, for fear you lose the taste for walking. Each integration, each comprehension, each time you gain a wider and deeper awareness is but a stop-over that is more or less comfortable on your journey. You may stop there for as long as you wish, but sooner or later, in this life or another, you will have to get going again.

Anyway, more than the route you take, it is the intent you carry which matters: at the end of the day, all your meanders and detours are of little importance. Each of us has within himself/herself, this compass that leads towards her/his luminous *I*.

Once this destination is clarified, this *I* at the highest of yourself, just put it in your pocket to retrieve it from to time, let yourself be guided by life. By encounters, books, events, adventures and these little things that do a lot. You will discover that Life is alive, it knows perfectly well what it does, where it takes you as long as you let her do.

Alive!

We have to tell this ourselves every day: it is in life that it all happens and nowhere else. It is precisely made for that: to act and be in awareness.

What is lived in *presence* is real, particularly our emotions, sensations, intents.

Every one of us knows the incredible power of emotions, the irresistible authority with which they take possession of our beings. One usually gets washed away. To live is to experience and endure the force of what inhabits us and try to get along with it. It is to **experience the unmeasurable power of the living,** which obtrudes itself upon us, whatever we do. The power of Intent to be and of the Sense of being all at once, which is unreservedly greater than what we are.

The essence, the purpose, the reality feeds off what we live, what we experience, when done *in awareness,* this is the reason of our coming into this world. The awareness field that begets and surrounds what happens to us, the events we go through, the encounters we make, all these things we have always been around for as long as we can remember.

Our acts.

Everything is an opportunity to make an *act of presence*, to *gain awareness.*

Engage in the living! Live your life fully not sparsely. Make it an experience of total awareness to the fullest.
Drink, taste, smell, touch life, be overwhelmed by it, love it. Without forgetting what you are at the deepest of yourself.

Both fully within and totally detached, immersed as well as a witness.

All at the same time.

At our human scale, quite the same experience as the *One-Presence*'s.

To perform an act is the vessel of the living, of the divine. Each time one thinks or expresses an intent, one creates, one engages into an act [1].

Our awareness, our being only evolves and transforms by what is proven and felt through experience. **What we know is only as worthy as what we do with it.** Experience is what makes us move forward, every scientist knows that. Otherwise, knowledge is useless at best, a hindrance at worse.

To think, to design, to act actualises your *presence field*, it makes you experience a very specific part of Reality. The whole perfection of it appears when, from then on, as you witness the effect of your intents and acts upon others and yourself, you let the impulse for a change rise deep within.

To perform an act is the most beautiful worship that can be.

---

[1] See page 207

But let us not make the journey before we get started. All will come in due time, and you may just take the above as a taster of what is to come.

I Am-ness

The *Presence* fields of Creation

-

The story at the beginning told us something: all is awareness, everything is *presence*. From this derives a Reality that we are unaware of most of the time. **Whatever you lay your consciousness upon, whatever you focus your mind on, grows each time in importance, to the point that it eventually becomes your reality.** This is a fact of existence, a fact of life, an inherent law of Creation.

There is a truly extraordinary game, a vertiginous feed-back loop that is so perfectly made, between your *presence* plane that defines the ingredients of a "reality" and the response you get from the experience you make of this reality, which unceasingly confirms and enriches your very own sense of being. This endless loop forms a stable and dynamic equilibrium which we call reality. It happens at every awareness field within Creation. Something like a gigantic video game where you can choose the level at which to play, with plenty of lives for that.

Our lives, each of the lives of any being, result from a living combination of awareness degrees that is specific to each and every of us. Each circumstance that we create and live is an opportunity to act from our awareness field and act upon it in return, either reinforcing it or broadening it so as to change.

Just try this out. Take any event that happens to you or that you are part of, and see how it is an opportunity to immediately distinguish between different realities, different ways of taking things, different orders at work. In this way, you allow your *presence* plane to confirm itself or you reach out to new ones. Conversely (and this is key, because it works both ways), the *presence* plane from which you operate defines very precisely the circumstances that come to you, that happen to you. **Therefore, if you truly want to understand what happens to you, it is vital to acknowledge the various awareness fields that form your sense of being.**

Now is the time to describe them as precisely as possible.

These are powerful and dynamic driving forces, **each one is useful and necessary**, each one makes it possible for the *One-Awareness* to experience a given degree of itself, with its own purpose, qualities and features. Each is but an expression of Creation from its own perspective. It is crucial to realise that whatever the presence degree, each one serves Creation in its own particular way. **Each awareness degree is a level of service.** This is precisely what makes them so powerful.

In that sense, inasmuch we understand their role and place, they are no obstacle or mistake on our way, they are just realities we are not quite aware of and do not understand yet. Each one defines a realm of its own that perfectly matches its purpose and our problems arise when we take their world for ours or when we get confused with their purpose.

Each awareness field integrates into the fields "above" it, which enables the latter *to act with it and within it.* Thus, the three first ones (mineral, vegetal, animal) are auxiliaries, partners, tools for us, human beings, they are our companions provided that we learn how to use them *in full awareness.* These *presence* degrees are inherent to us, inseparable from who we are. Our organs and senses are sensitive to their frequencies, because they are precisely made for perceiving them, *comprehending* them. These *presence* levels are **in us** just as well as around us, which makes it possible for us to *know them,* organise and use them. If they were not, we would not detect them and would not know what to do with them. At every moment, we choose to express this or that aspect of their nature according to our own natures and inclinations, and this defines the array and nature of the experiences we can access.

Therefore, in order to live our humanity fully, in order to make our choices in full awareness, we must identify and understand which awareness fields our own *presence* state is made of, what we do to/in the world we live in.

We must constantly identify and understand what drives us to act, what are our very own fabric ingredients, what operates in us, so as to try and "clear the signal from the noise". Then, we will gradually experience in this world the benevolent glow of a truly humane nature: prosperity, abundance, perfect satisfaction of all needs, attention, care, protection and recognition **for all beings**, whether humans or the underlying *presence* levels of Creation.

There are seven awareness degrees, natures, realms, planes or fields of *presence* or forces, each of them being organised across its own levels[1]. Any of these terms may be use alternatively as they are somehow equivalent. Speaking of forces has some benefits: it helps to perceive their dynamic and vibrating nature, their active power, their capacity of influence too. Speaking of planes or realms makes it possible to understand that at each level of Creation there exists a whole program, a universe, with its own functions, degrees, laws and aspirations.

The first four ones define our manifested world, the world of substance that is perceptible to our senses. The three "next" ones are part of the unmanifested realms, which we cannot perceive except when it happens that our senses awake to them and are inspired by them[2].

- The most basic, the crudest one is the material *presence*.
- The next is the vegetal *presence*.

---

[1] Awareness is like temperature: its variation is continuous, with thresholds where it shifts from one state to another: for example, according to temperature, water is solid (ice) then liquid then vaporises.

[2] Bear in mind though that even these four first levels have unmanifested realms (the « spirits »).

- The next is the animal *presence.*
- Then comes the fourth realm of *presence,* the ordinary human, our physical/psychic form, the *manifested human being,* who cannot be separated from the fifth one:
- The nature of the *Real[1] Human,* the Anthropos, the Kingdom.
- The sixth and seventh *presence* realms are considerably subtler awareness vibrational frequencies and will be touched on at a later stage.

Awareness is inclusive: these *presence* degrees are intricated worlds like matryoshkas[2]. Each one exists in its own autonomous way but is embedded in or linked to and constantly interacts with the others (nothing is separated in Reality).

-

This results in several consequences:

---

[1] Real because it is part of Reality, while the ordinary human is part of the « necessary illusion » of separateness.

[2] *"The Saviour said, all nature, all formations, all creatures exist in and with one another, and they will be resolved again into their own roots. For the nature of matter is resolved into the roots of its own nature alone. He who has ears to hear, let him hear.* » (The Gospel of Mary ch.4 – 22-24)

- All properties and qualities of a *presence* plane (awareness degree) are contained in all those beyond, which enables these to know them. One could say that, within the continuous exchanges between awareness degrees, each degree assimilates (knows) and transcends (raises) those who are "below ".
- Each *presence* degree can act within the ones it accesses or contains. It is therefore able to orientate, organise, inspire, raise them.
- The (physical) human being is precisely at the hinge between the manifested/"separated" worlds and the non-separated/subtler ones.

At this stage, you may understand that the tensions, existential conflicts of interest or belief that run through us and through our societies are but tensions between awareness degrees *within* us, and therefore *between* us [1].

---

[1] What is outside mirrors the inside, the more separated inside, the more dispersed outside, the more unified inside, the more united outside.

The first *presence* degree: the material nature [ix]

«Attachment to the material
generates an unnatural passion.
Disorder then appears throughout the body
This is why I am telling you
"Be in harmony
if you become unadjusted
get inspiration from the representations
Of your true nature." » [x]

The order of matter is the elementary *presence* plane, the basic frequency of Creation.

It is the force that makes things hold. Its purpose is to hold the manifested world. The material *presence* supports, holds, retains, contains, possesses, guards. This is the power of stone. Its function is **inflexibility**. It is the most irredeemable expression of Creation, the field of the strongest resistance. It is of relentless rigour; it wants itself immutable and this immutability holds our world. It is easy to understand the need for it.

The material *presence* is gradual, it extends from the crudest "realities" (stone, metal) to more elaborated or even subtle ones (water, air).

This rudimentary *presence* plane is limited to its sole sense of self, nothing else. Nothing else exists but self. **The world of a material being is reduced to itself.**

Self and nothing else. In that way, at least, one is certain not to move.

"*I Am-ness*" at its simplest, in its rawest and most immovable sense. An immovable *I*, the gravity of the heaviest stone.

It knows nothing of the *presence* of the other, it has no awareness of it whatsoever.
If you put two glasses one next to the other, each has a sense of being, each is filled with an acute awareness of its purpose which it will fulfil without fail, always the same way and no other. In this instance, to contain. **They can only execute what they are made for**, in the utmost immutability. What would a glass be if it started to wiggle about on its own? But none is aware of the other glass presence, let alone of the environment around. They are unaware that they are moved around or filled, not even of the liquid temperature. For this,

one would need other things, sensors, each with a dedicated function.

A thing equals a purpose.

Thus, individuals who mainly develop within this *presence* degree[xi] exhibit an **absolute and principled inflexibility**, something of the order of gravity. Nothing distracts them from their route, from their task or the mission they believe they have been entrusted with. Whatever their acts, they have no concern for their consequences whatsoever. They apply the rule, the law or the contract to the letter. They are their own and unique justification, without any consideration for the effects of their actions. They are unable to take the other into account, who he/she/it is, what they think, what they feel, what their needs are, let alone their aspirations.

This translates into dictatorships in the political arena, into dominance of money in social relationships, into systematic processes within organisations. In our lives, it expresses through the overwhelming mechanical rigour of machines and timetables.

Since money is mentioned, let us stop there for a while. Money has the rigour and immutability of matter: whoever has been in debts knows the unremitting weight of the money owed. Money has been conceived by humans to enable **exchanges**, consequently this force which we created is compelled to constantly circulate. Money never stops circulating[1]. In the same way as a glass is made for containing, money moves around. All the time. Even the money you spare *"has to work"* and the banknotes which possibly sleep in hiding under one's mattress will sooner or later wake up and circulate in their turn, if only because a thief will come and steal them [2]. You may therefore understand how difficult it is to retain, not to spend it. To spend is merely to make it possible for money to fulfil its purpose. In order to use money for one's benefit and according to its purpose, one does not hold it, one puts it *at work.*

Any material object is compelled to fulfil the function it was created for, what is engrained in its sense of being, in the intent that prevailed when it was conceived. Whether it is money, a car, a

---

[1] Cf. the utter nonsense of nano-transactions on the stock market.

[2] In this instance, the thief, whose mind is fully occupied by money matters, is but a tool for money to circulate again.

phone, a computer or a weapon. Whoever owns an object, must accept to be continuously subjected to this pressure and to take responsibility[1] for the acts that derive from this object's sense of being, as defined by its purpose: the tenacious intent to be used.

To own is to learn to master and it is advisable to wisely dose what you can own and master.

In a world that is immerged within the *presence* of matter, every being including human is perceived in terms of utility, everything is but a tool[2]. *I take what I find useful, I discard what is not.* The other, whoever he/she may be, is either an obstacle to be removed, eliminated if necessary, or a means to be used, because everything must contribute to one's own sense of being, nothing may stand in the way.

The industrial revolution has generalised in the world, this perception of humans as utilities. All that which workers have been asked for, for decades if not centuries, were yields, quality and

---

[1] Taking *responsibility* is our way, as human beings, to acknowledge the law of cause and effect in this world, the unescapable unity between the doer, the act and its effects.

[2] One speaks of human "resources".

schedules according to standards, all principles that exclusively belong to the realm of matter. These principles still live on today, but they begin to be complemented, even replaced by creativity, initiatives, flexible organisations, innovation which are proper human features, while yield, performance and quality are being entrusted to robots, which goes along with their material nature.

When one is under the influence of the material *presence*, owning an object or money reinforces one's sense of being. At this awareness degree, we must always have the latest version, the fastest car, the largest number of rooms, the biggest jewels, the most expensive brands, the biggest bank account, ...

The material *presence* has two effects upon humans: to retrieve satisfaction from what is owned, **which gets increasingly shorter** and rapidly **transforms into habit and right**, together with the irrepressible longing to have more. Sooner or later, more is necessary: a second or third car, a tenth pair of shoes, a pool, three houses, an aeroplane, the latest generation of anything. For beings under this influence, no belonging is enough, one always needs more.

From then on, the *Intent to Be/Sense of Being*, as it expresses in human beings inhabited by the material *presence*, creates people who are artificially happy and profoundly unhappy, as the insatiable urge to possess irremediably turns into lack while the weight of things grows in proportion. The balance becomes increasingly tensed between the desire that pushes and gravity that refrains[1]. One thinks the lack is filled with even more possessions while, in fact, one is caught in a loop of increasingly narrow and pressing confinements.

Therefore, in the world of matter, the "have" outshines the "be"; to have becomes to be, they blend to the point of merging. Owning is by far the dominant impulse in this *presence* degree. One exists by what one owns, much more than by what one does, sees, smells, listens to, touches, gives or receives. As this material awareness degree has a nature of **immutable normality**, it is easy to understand how difficult it is to set free from this confinement (*"it has always been that way, this is in man's nature"* ...).

---

[1] Which is precisely the reproduction of the primal tension within the Source at the matter awareness degree.

Hence, for those submitted to the influence of the material force, there is a compelling need that nothing changes, that things remain as they are, with a strong **resistance to change**, to any movement, any evolution. This is the dictatorship of static, of the current state of affairs, of what has been acquired without the ability to consider the evolution of consciousness, of practices and usage. Only what exists now has any value, the future has none for a force that ignores otherness as well as movement. Yet life is change. Even mountains erode, even atoms transform in their own time, which is much, much slower than ours.

For these people, an immense need for **immobility and security** follows suit. Security becomes a constant worry, a condition that is essential for a living.

As it ignores movement, time and space, another influence of this force may be found in our need for **immediacy**. A human being within this awareness field wants it all right away. It becomes "natural" to do or get things even faster, instantly if possible.

Do a search about anything with your favourite search engine: you will be shown the time the machine took to display the answer (e.g., 0.53 sec.). What value has this information? How important is it to have the answer so promptly, and more to the point, what is the intrinsic value, the real content of an information delivered in such a short time? In another area, some internet delivery services take pride in their 24/7 one-day performance. Is it *really* useful? Cannot we wait any longer? Cannot we take, again, time in our lives, find pleasure in the waiting, in the anticipation, in events that are deferred? In trusting that it will eventually arrive whatever time it takes?

Automatism is yet another of this *presence* manifestations that weights most heavily upon human beings. The unique, immediate link, with no nuances, between the cause and the effect. Automatism mixed with inflexibility creates a world of machines, a world of matter where man searches for his real place. What is humane is ignored, crushed, disregarded. In our present world, logics, systems, automatisms are all expressions of materialism, and it is easy to understand the affinity of this force with our intellect, especially the Western one, for which logic and the weight of what is written is one of the pillars of society. Yet there exist around the world cultures with fuzzier logics, where one plus one does not necessarily equal two, depending on the context. There exist cultures which are more humane, more supple and adaptative, where what happens one day may be different the next one, according to circumstances. Societies where ownership is not appropriate.

One of the most brutal expressions of this *presence* plane, which inflicts the most suffering to the beings who are subjected to it, is the **commoditisation of the living**. It is more or less apparent, perceptible, insidious. As an example, it has been long since man turned animals into objects to the point of having totally mechanised their *"exploitation"*, of manufacturing (!) breeds and races, of inflicting shameful treatments in breeding and rearing processes, in slaughterhouses[1]. To the point of having **knowingly if not wilfully** reduced, if not turned extinct, the extraordinary diversity of species, whether vegetal or animal.

The commoditisation of the living happens just as much among humans, especially in the relationships at work[2] or between genders: a woman becomes a thing, a male possession, an

---

[1] Further on, we will see that animals are able to feel and have emotions!

[2] The human exclusively reduced to the function he/she is assigned to.

79

"object" of desire and lust (some speak of "possessing" a woman), or the different ways of exploiting the human body whether female (most often) or male.

Observe our world, see the multiples forms under which this vibrational awareness field expresses, how **its grip upon our lives has become the "normal course of things" (!)**, the disproportionate presence of machines, the extent to which we have become dependent on them, or the relentless pressure of economics, by which we force our lives in a direction that is not humane.

Then we can have a feel of the colossal influence of the material *presence* upon us. It is one of the most active and most perceptible ones in our world today. We are immersed in the material, whether it be our buildings, roads, cars, things, all that we have created with **our mind, which has a very strong and totally addictive affinity to this awareness plane.**

Our mind is made for designing, differentiating, developing and creating, and it most cases, we need materials to create. It is in the realm of substance that mankind expresses its ability to create in the most spectacular way. **Apart from**

rare exceptions, human beings focus almost exclusively their intelligence on material achievements. Whether in technique, industry, research and now medicine, even in music and the arts[1], matter has become the support of choice for the human genius. To the point that many of us do not even imagine how it would be possible to create without a material support. To the point that those in this awareness state, *"do not know what to do"* when inactive. They are constantly restless, obsessed with the need to do something, which for them is the natural expression of their sense of being and the shortest route to the satisfaction of having.

This quasi-exclusive focus considerably reinforces the grip of matter upon our intellect, hence upon our destiny.

It defines our reality.

In this regard, it is not necessary to dwell upon the consequences of our being fascinated and dependent upon our screens, televisions, smartphones, computers, tablets and gaming consoles. Thus, in our so-called "affluent" western societies, the time passed in *being absorbed* by

---

[1] With the exception of poets, dancers, actors, singers... all those who create with nothing.

machines is between seven to ten hours per person per day in average[1], that is between a third and a half of our waking hours. Every day, humans are more entangled in the universe of their artefacts, subjects of desire, adoration and fascination[2]. In such conditions, it does not come as a surprise that "humans" have sexual relationships with objects and soon machines.

This bond between the human mind and the material *presence* plane is very beneficial to the latter: while, according to its nature, it cannot develop nor move[3], it now can expand far beyond its natural boundaries. The human mind is the way by which the material *presence* can satisfy the *intent to be* within any being: to develop, multiply, deploy. Without the human intelligence, there would be on Earth only mountains, air, water, all

---

[1] An adult in Western societies – children and teenagers spend between 4 to 7 hours a day in front of a screen, outside of school-related activities.

[2] As a proof, look around when in the tube, at a bus stop, on the train: nearly everybody is absorbed by his/her smart(!)phone. It is nearly impossible to do without it, otherwise one gets bored, one is not.

[3] Except under its most subtle forms such as air and water, or at its atomic or astronomical levels.

the material entities that are present in nature. Instead, we have considerably multiplied them under many forms, including beyond our planet.

This situation is totally out of control and weighs heavily upon the human destiny, it drags it down to the plane of matter, instead of letting it be aspired (inspired) towards higher *presence* degrees. These may even become subjects of mockery, laughable illusions for anyone under the influence of matter. They speak of hairy-fairies, dreamers, worlds of nursery rhymes...

We are thus given to understand how a *presence* field that is fully part of Creation, with a place, a role and a purpose of its own, can lead us astray, divert us from our very own nature, when we allow it to permeate our own *presence* field to the point of substituting for it.

Unbeknownst to us, our perception is altered and our whole way of being is modified: our awareness, our intents, our objectives, our acts vibrate only in the material *presence* field.

What was a deviation becomes the new normal and what is of our real nature becomes illusion. The world thus created by human beings (we will see how further on) becomes a world of lack, of gravity and enslavement, a world of ignorance and suffering as the gap widens between what we truly are and what we give ourselves to live.

The second *presence* degree: the vegetal nature[xii]

The Vegetal Force is a *presence* vibration that is more elaborate than the material one. At this level, one usually begins to speak of a life form[1].

To begin with, one must understand that, as it feeds upon mineral components, the vegetal *presence* field assimilates the qualities of the mineral realm and makes them its own; it consequently is determined and persistent.

There is however a significant difference between the mineral and vegetal states: while the first is inert and devoid of senses, the latter has the capability to sense, it is endowed with **sensations.** As we know now[xiii], vegetal entities experience

---

[1] Even though the interactions between air, water, stone, the earth movements and the gigantic exchanges of energies within the cosmos are life forms at the material level.

sensations, but these are not associated with emotions. Each vegetal being is equipped with several biological sensors able to detect a movement, a colour, a temperature, light or pressure, hence, to communicate and trigger the adequate reaction. If you damage it, when an insect crawls on a leaf, the vegetal entity senses it and sets up a signal or an adapted reaction. For example, a self-defence response, emission of poison, a spasmodic reflex, self-healing etc. Whilst living, it can turn to light or heat, or extend its reticulated networks towards water or nutrients that it senses in the distance and which it needs.

Thanks to this ability to sense, the vegetal order is aware of "the other", of **otherness**, of what is around. It understands it is not alone in the world, it is conscious of its environment and particularly of what is useful, beneficial or dangerous. Hence, the vegetal has developed the means of apprehending its environment, to benefit of it and to protect itself, as with thorns, poison, hair, height or the roughness of a trunk to protect its fruits etc.

Like all that has been created from the Source, the vegetal realm, in all its varieties, is impregnated with *intent to be and sense of being*. This awareness enlivens it with an innate sense of purpose. This purpose is to **survive** as well as to contribute to its own development and to the world's by **nourishment**. This duality at the core of the vegetal *presence* can easily be observed. Just take a fruit: the seeds (survival) are surrounded by flesh (nourishment). The flesh is used to nourish the seed and start its growth, and at the same time it contributes to nourishing the world, to which the seed can also be used in most cases.

Survival and nourishment are found in the prodigious prodigality that the vegetable realm demonstrates: how many grains on a single ear of wheat, on a sunflower, in a squash, a pomegranate or a watermelon, how many grains of pollen on the stamen, how many acorns each year under an oak tree? Survival and nourishment may even be found in the decay of plants which, in turn, produces a fertile and nourishing humus in an endless circle.

Vegetal beings have developed a powerful cognitive capability that is perfectly fitted to their world. Trees, for instance, communicate between themselves about predator attacks, whether parasites, fungi or humans. In the vegetal world, all beings communicate.

This vital instinct (survive and nourish) materialises into three essential features which constantly show in this world:

- The first is the **need for growth**. Whoever has ever tended a garden, a field or a forest, may have experienced the phenomenal propensity of vegetal to grow, to develop, to extend. The plant is obsessed with the need to grow. Consequently, this innate and irrepressible need appears quite early in the organisation of the living. It is nearly a primary function, in direct relation with its survival instinct. When one observes trees, one may witness the fierce competition that forms between them in order to access light, oxygen, water and nutrients, especially in depleted environments. Of course, there exist cooperation forms between species and plants, that are subordinate to the need for survival, but **competition** is omnipresent, to the point where it is common for plants to choke each other or to survive at each other's expense in small or confined spaces. This need for expansion has led plants to develop expansion strategies that demonstrate, if need be, their cognition, their fine and adaptative knowledge of their environment: some plants (which, by nature, cannot move around) have organised the extension of their territory by way of devices using air or water, by being carried away or even ingested by animals to move their seeds around[1].

- The second quality is its ability to **communicate and send out signals**, to **weave networks**; that is a very powerful and highly developed sensitive and ramified capacity which comes next in its survival conditions. The reticular network of plants can extend very far or deep and we still know very little about how these networks convey information, especially between species[2].

- The third quality that strongly differentiates plants from the mineral level is their ability to **reproduce.** Plants have developed an

---

[1] This plant ability to have its seeds transported by the digestive system of animals is named *zoochory*, it is a truly amazing capability. It has to feel the presence of animals in its environment, to infer their nature, their behaviour and the way they operate so as to comprehend how to use them for its own development. For example, the rosehip develops fruits with attractive colours, whose ripening in late autumn corresponds to a period of scarcity for animals. Foxes (or birds) eat these fruits, move around and their droppings allow the rosehip to expand its territory. The same process is used by mistletoe, hawthorn or ivy.

[2] The intense and well organised cooperation between the roots of trees and mycelial networks is just being explored.

unequalled resourcefulness to ensure their reproduction, at the core of their survival purpose[1]. How the seed is protected against weather conditions or predators, its ability to keep its growing capability and nourishing power beyond centuries, conditions permitting, its ability to adapt to environmental changes, all of this demonstrate how carefully vegetables tend their reproduction and survival.

Stemming from these capabilities and purpose, the vegetal has developed the **need to compare**, so that it constantly evaluates its survival chances against those within its environment. From this, one may infer that vegetal species are **aware of their comparative superiority**. This should not be understood in the usual sense, rather as the capacity of the species to continuously evaluate its chances of growth, reproduction and survival, compared with those of other species, or individuals of its own species.

As soon as the awareness of otherness appears, the need to compare emerges. Indeed, in this

---

[1] See for instance how flowers use bees to carry their pollen from one plant to another, a much more efficient and targeted mean than the wind.

presence field that is aware of others, the intent to be that translates into the urge for growth inevitably triggers the need to master **competition** and defend oneself against it.

These features will be found in human beings under the influence of the vegetal *presence* plane[xiv], which has a particular kinship with our **desires**:

- An insatiable appetite for **growth.** Our enterprises, our consumer society are founded on the dogma of imperative growth: to survive is to grow and one does not know how to survive without growth. If we place ourselves within the vegetal *presence* plane, a world without growth is unthinkable (including growth at the material level which is a nonsense somehow), even though our human intelligence tells us we live in a world of finite resources. This urge for growth resonates in human beings with their constant craving for more. We have created a sort of ratchet effect where it is virtuous to grow, to have more and do everything never to have less, while this is precisely in the order of the living: life alternates more and less, up and down, hot and cold, dry and wet, life and death.

- The need to **constantly expand one's territory and to protect it,** in order to ensure the control of resources. This need has given rise to empires whether economical, ideological or political, to all forms of colonisation and to the resulting domination conflicts.

- The **sense of superiority** is likely what has the most shaped our ways of being and of interacting with our fellow humans. When we are under the influence of the vegetal awareness, we see the world and the others through an inferior/superior prism, from a hierarchical perspective of things and beings which is mostly in line with accessing resources.[1] Those who master this access consider themselves as "superior" as much as they consider "inferior" those to whom this access is denied. This leads "naturally" to setting up laws, norms and standards which serve those who master this access and make possible (and legitimate) to limit it or even exclude those deemed "inferiors".

---

[1] Be they land, agriculture, forest, water, mines, finances, education...

- From this feeling of superiority, humans under the influence of this force have naturally developed the **sense of competition**, of mastering a territory between groups or individuals (be it physical, economic, political, social, normative or dogmatic), which is an exact mirror of what happens between vegetal species. This competition may become a matter of life and death, would the environment become constrained (e.g. economical, climatic, political, social crises). This fierce competition combined with the insatiable urge of owning, results in the saying *"the winner takes it all"*, a situation that is much desired and designed to last, by the people impregnated by this force[1]. In a forest, it is easy to spot places that are totally colonised by a species, where nothing else grows, except dependent or companion species that are useful to the survival of the dominant.
- Under the influence of this force, one constantly feels the **need to compare**.

---

[1] There are people who are not surprised let alone ashamed by the fact that 26 individuals own as much as the poorer half of mankind, which is approximately 3,8 billion people.

Most often, this takes forms that are apparently innocuous, such as our "natural" inclination to judge or evaluate[1]. Other more insidious practices such as gossiping, criticizing, slandering, all of which indirectly make the other person belittled or vulnerable, are also of a vegetal nature. They are some sort of *poison,* a defensive or aggressive reaction, an attempt to grow and defend oneself at the expense of the other. Slander undermines the status of the other, nullifies him or her, corrupts him or her like an acid or a fungus.

- Under the influence of this force, we have developed the need to save and **to accumulate**; when one lives at this awareness plane, one constantly needs to stockpile, to build reserves up in anticipation of scarce tomorrows: because the plant perceives the seasons and their cycle, it stores nutrients because of its acute awareness of the variability and impermanence of its environment. The early agricultural societies did not fail to concern themselves about these matters and we keep many traces in us of this not-so-distant past. Some of us, reading this,

---

[1] See on page 225

may think *"but this is normal! This is sound practice!"*. Perhaps, but such an instance is an indication that we are still immersed in the vegetal *presence* or have not taken enough distance with it, so as to *know* that it is in the nature of the living to provide for everything we may need when we are at our proper place.

- Lastly, the vegetal force gives us the ability **to cooperate** between social groups or individuals. As one speaks of "companion plants or species", likewise we may consider the many agricultural coops, the various forms of alliance or even "coopetition" between social groups and enterprises.

We assimilate the vegetal *presence* plane in a very simple way: we feed on it. We constantly ingest nutrients that are specific to the vegetal world (proteins carbohydrates, lipids, vitamins...) which indeed are necessary to our own... survival and growth. We absorb at the same time the minerals (the material plane) which plants previously nourished themselves with.

Consequently, our body is mostly of a vegetal order as it builds upon and is maintained with plants. In the same way, we can heal and repair it mostly with vegetal condensates or essences. Which is what the first civilisations had already discovered, which in their majority lived at this *presence* degree.

When we eat, the vegetal essences that we ingest meet those in our body. If they do not match, it results in unease feelings and illness may occur. When a human being is attentive to this sort of things, when she listens to her body, she only eats what corresponds to the balance of essences within her at a specific time, which manifests in the need to eat this or that. Of course, this drive must be free from addictions, influences or sways.

When the outer and inner energies merge, if they match, it feels like a celebration. For the human being first, who feels a deep sense of pleasure and well-being, a sense of delight mixed with surprise that goes far beyond satiety (*"God, this is good!"*). Next, for the vegetal form of *presence* as well, for which this encounter feels like a climax, the equivalent of our carnal encounters.

Here we may understand the extent to which our diet directly relates to our health. We may understand just as well how a human being who poorly masters this *presence* field, will have a compulsive or frenetic need to eat a lot or often, to eat fast, only because the vegetal essences in him have the need to renew this experience as often as possible[1].

Be aware of how you eat, you will know where you are in your journey.

Because of this intimate proximity with our body, the vegetal *presence* vibration profoundly and powerfully resonates with our own sensations, how we *feel*. If we become aware of this affinity, we can no longer surprise at habits we have developed. For example, to have a little drink when tired or depressed, or conversely when it is party time, and we want to feel good and enjoy it. The need to light a cigarette when one is nervous or concerned, to smoke pot to feel cool and relax, or to take medicines when depressed.

The plant essences that man has learnt to condense or isolate in alcohol, tobacco, perfumes, medicines or drugs are extremely powerful awareness vibrations, with deep and lasting effects whether in the areas of health, pleasure, desire, addiction or alienation of will. Anyone who stopped smoking knows how strongly this force

---

[1] This is the reason why fasting may be a useful exercise provided it does not lead to gluttony when it ends.

can take over our consciousness and how difficult it is to detach from it. The same is true of alcohol or drugs.

Talking about these things is, by no means, a value judgment opposing a social or behavioural norm to another. Everyone is free and responsible to build the life experience he or she wants. Nevertheless, it is beneficial to do so in awareness, to understand what is happening within us, the causes and consequences on others and on ourselves, on the reality we shape, on our equilibrium and our aspiration (or not) to reach wider awareness degrees.

The third *presence* degree: the animal nature[xv]

It is easy to understand that the animal world benefits in its turn from the features of the awareness fields "below" it, i.e. the mineral and vegetal ones, as animals feed on plants and minerals when they eat or drink (including when they are carnivorous as they feed on herbivores and insects).

In addition, it has qualities of its own which enable it to live its life in a way that suits its own purpose.

Thus, with the animal realm, we move away from the elementary forms of creation and reach to a more complex *presence* vibration, closer to our own. These qualities are transmitted to us when we, in turn, feed on animals[1].

- Just like the mineral or vegetable world, animals have a **sense of being** as individuals, which can express powerfully (see for example the violence of fights between males). Animals sense what they are with strength and pride: they **know** they are agile, fast, powerful, beautiful, flexible, determined, efficient, careful, silent and they take a deep satisfaction in this.
- Like plants, animals are endowed with sensations, with the ability to sense but, in addition, they are endowed with feelings, with the ability to experience **emotions**. Thus, apart from the sense of danger, animals have the notion of pleasure or displeasure, of joy, boredom or sadness, of

---

[1] We even ingest animal forms without noticing: viruses or germs that surround us by the thousands and which we absorb, are essences of the animal realm. Essence = the most powerful content under the most minute form.

affection or mistrust. They have a deep sense of their worth and are therefore capable of pride, to the point, for example, of feeling challenged by a simple glance. Because of these emotions, animals know desire and fear, aggressiveness and, as a result, they can feel the strong impulses that we know such as happiness, envy, passion or anger. They too experience maternal or paternal love and family bonds. In the same way as sensations bring together plants and animals, emotions are a channel between animals and human beings, and it is often through the exchange of emotions that we communicate with them. Moreover, it is the emotion animals feel in the other that triggers an appropriate reaction.

- From this sense of being combined with the determination they inherit from the mineral realm via plants or water, animals have developed powerful capacities of volition, **willpower, resilience and courage** which serve their survival instinct (received from the vegetal field as well).

- A more elaborate awareness of their environment enables them to develop an **intelligence**, a cognitive capacity that corresponds to their *presence* plane as well as survival instinct: animals can observe, learn, understand the world they live in and take advantage of it. They can communicate, know languages (warn about predators, attract females or males, tell the direction of food[1]...), they are endowed with memory as well as anticipation of the future, they are capable of reasoning and categorising (pigeons can recognise forms, dogs, bears or even butterflies recognise smells from far, monkeys can reproduce complex processes. Cockatoos or crows may be seen making tools to catch larvae under the bark[2]). Of course, these cognitive abilities are precisely fitted to their environment and needs, and it does not take long generally for an animal to reproduce an act or process that allowed another to access food.

- These emotions and intelligence usually relate to two basic needs: food and sex,

---

[1] Cf the dance of the bee.

[2] New Caledonian crows cut the slice of indented leaves to dig in termite mounds. A crow in a laboratory has been seen twisting a wire and using it to fetch a cashew nut at the bottom of a tube.

with the related consequences: the **organization in society** (pack, herd, clan, colony) and the sense of pre-eminence and power that defines the **dominance** of individuals or species over others.

- Similarly, animal have developed an acute consciousness of their territory, which draws from the vegetal but which they amplified: they are able to create, relocate, define, organise and defend the territories, sometimes very vast, which they took ownership of for hunting, breeding as well as playing and relaxing.

- The animal force is an awareness of **dominance and predation**: the order of animal species is defined according to which eats which. In addition to their ability to defend themselves which they draw from the vegetal realm, animals have the capacity to attack and aggress[1]. This ability to predate led carnivores to grow powerful weaponry such as claws, jaw and limb muscles, teeth. When they pounce upon a prey, they act with speed, swiftness, precision and determination. The animal

---

[1] A clan of monkeys may be seen *preparing* and executing a raid upon a neighbour clan, or buffaloes taking punitive action against lions after one of their calves had been killed.

life is consequently a life **on the alert,** with **vigilance** as a second nature, under the possible threat of a predator, according to the logic *"eat or be eaten[1]"*. Similarly, this ability to predate has a possibly critical influence upon their environment. Animals are generally aware of this and consume only what they need or relocate their feeding grounds to allow their environment to recover.

- In order to defend themselves or attack, animals have developed an acute **swiftness** capability. Speed and swiftness are features that are specific to the animal realm. Apart from certain species which do not have to go far to find staple food and are naturally slow, these qualities make it possible for animals to provide for their needs: birds while flying[2], lizards or snakes

---

[1] The sense of danger of animals is adjustable: a lioness may move around a herd of antelopes without frightening them if they feel she is satiated. They only get nervous if they sense she is in "hunting mode".

[2] Swallows can fly at up to 75mph, "Many birds routinely experience positive G-forces greater than 10 G and up to 14 G while select military aircrafts can withstand gravitational forces of 8-10 G" (www.sciencedaily.com)

on the ground, fish in the sea, wild beasts as well as their preys in the savannah, all depend on speed to survive.

- Animals organise themselves **in groups**, they cooperate to achieve their ends, to efficiently find sustenance or defend against predators. Suffice to observe, as an example, how schools of fish, colonies of bees, wasps, hornets or termites, wolves' packs, flights of migratory birds and so on behave ...One can even see animals interpose to help another species under attack or in trouble.

- Finally, the animal force is characterized by an **insatiable sexual need**. *Most often a male copulates without restraint, by a kind of spontaneous reflex that makes him take any female passing by whenever he feels like it. To the point, for example, that a male chicken, duck or rooster will cover any female to satisfy his need, regardless of whether she is his mother, grandmother, daughter or sister. Similarly, when a female is in heat, she will call any male, not resting until she is covered. This constant sexual appetite has led the male to acquire the most flattering appearances, the most ostentatious feather or fur, to favourably impress the female, to the point of*

> *forgetting his predators and putting himself in danger (which is particularly noticeable among birds)[xvi].*

Similarly, the female develops powerful pheromones to attract and retain the male even from a great distance.

Thus, by observing these things, we can understand how our own behaviours and patterns are more or less under the influence of the animal awareness plane [xvii].

- The need for **power, might and dominance** is one of its first expressions in our world. Humans who live within this awareness field, are used to saying phrases such as *"eat or be eaten, the law of the mightiest, the world is but a jungle, the survival of the fittest..."*, under a logic of predation, subservience and dominator/dominated relationships. What matters a show of muscles, literally and figuratively. They often refer to the animal world, if only to justify their deeds. (*"man is a wolf to man, I watched like a hawk, he took the lion's share, such a pig-head..."*).
- In another form, the need for power of an ego dominated by this influence expresses

by the need of **being right against the other**. Just have a look at what agitates you when you want to be or even think you are right. It expresses a defensive or dominating ego, immersed in the plane of animal awareness.

- The need for domination, when mixed with the aggression capability of the animal nature, brings forth the potential for **violence** that is found in the human under the influence of this force. When subjugated to this awareness field, humans may wound or even destroy the other whether physically or psychologically, so much so that some may even find pleasure in doing harm to others. The sickening levels of violence in human relationships, in our behaviours and conflicts, even our leisure, our games, sports and interest centres, tell us the extent to which we are collectively immersed within this degree of animal awareness vibration. Here again, the beings under this influence can only perceive the world through this prism: they will explain to whomsoever is willing to listen that it is in the nature of the world to be violent, it is the way it is, and it has always been so.

- The **sexual appetite** stemming from the animal awareness degree may drive those under its influence to not only multiply circumstances but partners and experiences too. This need for pleasure is irrepressible to the point that it becomes a way of life and people come to organise their lives in a way that satisfies it before any other consideration.

- Similarly, the need **to attract and seduce**, to get noticed comes from this very same *presence* field. How we put on perfumes, make-up, the way we dress, walk or simply look at the other, what attracts us in him or her, tell how far our being is under this influence. Here, the need to seduce, conquer, drag attention (or even impose oneself onto the other) is perceived as the "natural" expression of gender relationships. Every situation is lived according to the perspective of mutual attraction, and one's feeling of *I Am-ness* is based on the sole condition one pleases. How many men, women, youngsters feel belittled, negated, inexistant even, only because they do not feel they please? Are we the same when we wear elegant outfits or appealing attire as when our clothes are more common, less catchy, less fashionable or fitting?

- Human beings whose *presence* is immersed in this awareness realm will particularly concern themselves with their **vital space**, to protect their own territory. Closeness of the other is felt as an annoyance, an intrusion even. More than others, they are sensitive to neighbourhood disturbances or noises in the surroundings. On the contrary, for beings who let a genuine human *presence* arise within, these circumstances are an occasion to experience compassion, patience and a feeling of togetherness with the other. Where the first feel a hindrance or even let exasperation grow, the latter feel calm and at peace, which in turn engenders calm and peace around them.

- It goes without saying that the animal force is at the core of **our most primary impulses**: pleasure, satisfaction, anger, rage. How fast these emotions surge in ourselves and how well we can master them or not, are indeed precious indications of where we stand as regards this *presence* degree and to what extent it commands to our behaviours.

What can we do with these subhuman awareness degrees?

"People work with animals to plough their fields
and therefore are able to feed themselves
As well as animals, whether domestic or wild.
So it is with the Realised Human Beings, who work
with energies that obey them
They prepare all things to come into being.
Hence, everything awakens and is redeemed.
Good and evil, right and left.
The Breath leads all things to their repose,
It aligns the energies: the obedient, the wild and
the solitary.
It gathers them together so that
They are no longer dispersed."[xviii]

Pay attention

Pay attention, observe yourself and watch the world as it appears to you, as you live it. See the facets of what you are as parts of a living entity, the diversity expressed by Creation. Observe how intricate are the dynamics at work, how powerful are the forces at play within you as well as between us, in what you do, think or intent to. Be a witness of what is at work, what seeks to dominate. Identify within yourself the features of each of the forces we just mentioned. Endeavour, yes endeavour to pay real attention, to be as much as possible a vigilant and compassionate witness as well as participant, and try to only give way to what nourishes, empowers and soothes. When you express something different, examine wherefrom that comes and how attached you are to it. Acknowledge, identify but judge not.

This is an everyday exercise.

Every situation is an occasion to watch and understand yourself, to identify these active *presence* vibrations within you, wherefrom you act. **The good news is that it suffices to apply discernment to invite change into your reality**. Suffice to bring to your consciousness a new understanding of where your moods, acts, intentions come from, to let a broader and unattached perception of yourself grow.

There appears the choice to carry on with the experience at the level you started on or to open to the possibility to change for another. **No willpower is needed.** What it is all about is how to develop your ability to seize the full potential of the instant, **all the possibilities it is made of.**

Each moment is Creation re-enacted.

Every instant is a crux moment, undoubtedly each of them. But this moment when the consciousness may open, when the choice of another *presence* appears, is so light, so brief and elusive, as difficult to catch as a puff of wind, that, if not grasped, the dynamics of circumstances and habits promptly takes over and we carry on as usual with the scenario of our lives. If we train however, it soon becomes a habit, and life comes to our help.

Therefore, open yourself to the possibility of marvelling at the extraordinary intelligence at work within Creation, at its magnificent order and diversity. You truly need nothing or nobody, only silence maybe, to be enthralled by the beauty of a landscape, of a galloping herd in the savannah, by the flight of migratory birds, by the flavour of a fruit or the delicate scent of a flower. By jubilant conversations around tables or by the children's joy in the morning snow. And above all, by the stunning and profound beauty of how all these play together the fabulous game of Life. It tells the splendour of the world, of what we are given to experience. Allow yourself to be filled at the fullest, as you would with an exquisite perfume that you never tire of, never.

Here gratitude surges, clear, joyful and peaceful like a spring.

In this state of being, things will come to your mind, novel intuitions come to you. You are given the possibility to comprehend where the human *presence* stands in the vastness of Reality, in perfect balance between its crudest and highest expressions.

All is in due place.

These gradual *presence* degrees are perfect expressions of the Source. Each carries in its own specific way the primal *Intent to be* and *Sense of Being*. They are our fellow players. They are extremely powerful and fully aware of their being and purpose, all at once in their own realm and part of the formidable intensity of the human experience, all of us actors of Creation. Yet most of the time, we interact with them unknowingly, unaware of what *really* occurs between them and us.

Creation is immensely magnificent and orderly, and it is fitting, as regards our human journey, to understand where we stand in that order, what our role and place are. A house is made of foundations, walls and a roof. If the foundations take on the walls' role, we live in a cave. If the walls take on the roof role, we live in a manger. If the roof takes on the foundations' role, the house flies away in the next storm.

Is this really what we want?

These life forces have their proper reason for being in the world. **Each celebrates the Source in its own way**. As for us, witnesses and actors in turns, we need each of them to live (seen from the outside) as well as to grow (seen from the inside). We comprehend them (both in terms of inclusion and understanding) and ought to identify to what extend they are useful or necessary to us, how they express within us, what they have us do.

Just for a time, the time you will live on, or the shorter one as you read these pages, make yourself artisan of your life. Put a little order in your tools and materials. Understand how to use them in awareness, with love and respect. In mastery that is. A master artisan never entrusts his best tools to his apprentice, for fear he damages them or hurts herself. Become an apprentice of your life before you believe you master it. Before you act, carefully verify what drives you to act. Before you speak, check the intention your words carry. Pay attention to this man or woman you think you are and choose your tools and manipulate them accordingly.

Understand you are an apprentice.
Learn and realise.

Realise that each of these awareness fields is active, prodigiously active in its own essence. Whether we want it or not, it is part of ourselves, each of us, this is unescapable. They nest in our presence and never leave and, as soon as we think of them or make use of them, they grow. If we are not aware of them, they soon become driving forces.

The material nature is the force behind **our intelligence, our intellect.** It enables us to shelter, to protect ourselves, to build technologies, machinery and tools. It is the reason why we only think of the money we want to earn, save or spend, the house we wish to own, build or rent, the business we want to create or develop, the things we long for. It is behind our impatience, coldness and rigidity, it is the source of the violence we do to ourselves or to others.

The vegetal nature is the force behind our **desires**. It enables us to feed, feel, be healthy and get dressed. Besides, it is the cause of our constant need for comparison, of our arrogance and feeling of superiority. It is the reason for our avarice, gluttony and greed.

The animal nature is the force behind our **willpower and determination**. It gives us the courage to undertake and the energy to do. It is the motor of our ambitions, our angers, our fears and our passions, our sexual urges, the reason why we feel attacked and the need to defend ourselves, of our lust for power.

Each of these *presence* states is, at its very level, perfectly at its place within Creation. When in their world as well as when playing together, every species in each of these fields manifests a particular nature or form, a vibrational *presence* degree, rightly ordered within the immensely vast and harmonic diversity of Creation, the complete expression of the Source. Outside of their world, they wreak havoc. When in the jungle, an elephant majestically contributes to the order of its world. When in a china shop, it is a total disaster.

As an apprentice, observe and understand what inhabits you, what stirs and overwhelms you, all that your ego is made of. Comprehend the extent to which your preoccupations, desires and reactions which form what you believe you are, manifest a pile of tenacious and deeply engrained veils and filters that prevent you from perceiving and expressing your reality as a human being.

What you occupy yourself with, occupies you.
For us, these awareness fields are occupying forces.

Try and grasp the totality of what occupation means. You may be able then to discern the strange porosity of your senses, this fuzzy frontier between *I* and "the rest". When you look at a tree, be aware that its *presence* is already in you, otherwise you would not be able to see it. It goes the same when you contemplate a mountain, rejoice for a bird or watch a flock. Not to mention when you meet or think of other humans.

You can experiment it right here and now: look at a tree, a cloud or a hill, whatever landscape happens to be in your sight. You may feel it alive and vibrating within you, as an interiorised image, the exact mirror of what you are looking at.

We are what we see, hear, touch and sense. We become what we think of.
What is the artefact, what is the reflection? In which direction the mirror?

We are occupied by these energies and awareness fields, in every sense of it. Be aware of their *presence* and ask yourself: What am I doing with them? Am *I* driving the car or is the car driving me? Am *I* using money or is money using me? Who am *I* when *I* want?

A car that is made for driving fast, will **inevitably** entice you to make speed, it is in its very own nature, its purpose. Similarly, accumulated money is far more powerful that money in scarce quantity. Are you certain you master it?

All these envies, where do they come from?

And these worries?

Be aware that what you believe is outside is inside too. There actually is only an immense, sublime unified awareness field we wander in thanks to a disguise of our senses, like choices we ceaselessly make, unbeknownst.

Because we perceive ourselves as separated, we believe we master and are free of these forces that we see outside of ourselves. Whereas we are not and do not. They exist and live within us, resonate with our own *presence* field, so much so that we believe this is us.

When we master them poorly, they overwhelm us, and we experience the heaviness of things.
All our defences and projections, all our creeds and desires, our imagination, reflexes and impulses are so profoundly impregnated with these *presence* fields that they completely shroud our perception of our true nature and of Reality.
Such an ubiquitous noise that we perceive nothing or so little of the signal.

"The current state of human consciousness obstructs the flow of the Divine"[xix]

Surprise and ask yourself, put yourself in question more than in affirmation. Stow away all your convictions about who you are and about the world. This simple consciousness state is enough, this is the precise moment when you set off toward That, which you are and carries you. Toward the Source. Through this minute crack in your own sense of being, the Breath will pass, like a tiny breeze at first, then like a storm that will blow away everything you thought you were.

Just like the droplet of water which oozes through the dam, announces that, one day, it will collapse.

At this very moment, you find yourself.

Be in re-cognition

There is a powerful affinity between these vibrational fields, our intellect, desires and emotions, there would even be a competition between them, in order to determine which would drive what we want to do with ourselves.

Just like the competition for light or air between trees, for food or water between animals.

For a reason that is easy to comprehend: all that which is created, including the primitive awareness forms, is inhabited with the intent to be at its highest. Therefore, when they are used or assimilated by upper awareness planes, they participate in Creation at their own highest. In the exact same manner as plants naturally turn to light, we wish (a priori) to be inspired by wider awareness degrees.

It is thus of the utmost importance that you identify these fields, know them, appreciate, tame and organise them; that you enable them to work in *good intelligence*, not only from the "outside", which you daily do, but from the "inside" of yourself too. To clarify your intents, what enacts you.

Tidy up your workshop and do not think you know. Understand we all are humans in the making.

Do not fear mistakes but recognise when you make one. It is rather simple: it suffices to observe all the consequences of your deeds as well as to be aware of the intents and thoughts that were behind. All of them, not forgetting any. Examine the consequences upon others, upon the world and yourself and check them against your intentions.

Here we are learning our work as human beings, and this is precisely the reason why each of us came into this world: **quite simply because we are not done with these forces yet.**

Maybe have we not even started?

These *presence* fields have a reason for being, just as are human beings they are vibrational fields of the *One-Awareness* that created the world. Nothing can escape the Divine and, as such, they **deserve our respect**. Doing so, we recognise them at their very place and there are many benefits for the human condition in this world to use them and organise them *in awareness*.

If we respect these awareness levels for their functions and for what they are, if we recognise them in ourselves and put them at their place, if we use them while accepting, ourselves, to be used by higher awareness planes, then we acknowledge we are part of the *One-Awareness* in all its vibrational degrees and we may be assured that it is the beginning of a long and fruitful collaboration for us, humans, with all these fields.

Re-cognise their reason for being, be *in recognition* and gratitude, you will then hear their own voice, what each of these *presence* fields has to tell you and the qualities they bring to you, they will tell you how to savour and appreciate them, how to use them and your life will irrevocably change.

Use them

These forces are beautiful, efficient, powerful and to use them is a limitless source of satisfaction and marvel.

They are in labour! The whole Creation is in labour, in every sense of it. All the *presence* realms are at work, we know and experience this every day. Including the ones that are beyond our human level, which we cannot sense. It is in the Creation's nature, in the order of the universe, to work, that is to **make a *presence* level express its content by interacting with the vibrational planes and forces it can access.** This is quite exactly what to work means. This is precisely what plants do with minerals, what animals do with plants and minerals. What we do in our turn.

To work.
With. Within.

As we will soon see, the genuine work, the true act is selfless, clear of any egotistical intent[1]. One truly acts by letting oneself do, one acts *with* better than *upon*, under the guidance of circumstances more

---

[1] True work is disconnected from the idea of value and money. Its content, its intent has more reality than its result. See on page 207

than of will, moved by a wider source of inspiration.

Selfless acts proceed from Reality and in this process, **every *presence* field that is part of them, participate in Reality at its level** and *Reality* is what it is made for. Conversely, if performed from the ego, acts become illusions, foam, void. They are agitation, lost or dead. Wasted opportunities.

When you do not act from a human level but from an ego crammed with these forces, you (and therefore they) miss the point; their awareness-energy goes nowhere else than you and therefore accumulates in you. You become their destination and destiny. They weight upon you and lock you within their *presence* fields.

On the other hand, each time you act with no ego, when you question and check your motives to impede your lust for personal benefit and let your highest inspiration radiate, you merely become a channel and the awareness-energy of the *presence* fields you use joins the Reality continuum and dissipates in it. You channel them without being cluttered, you keep nothing and stay clear.

This is almost mathematical.

This is how important the labour-act is.

An act performed in awareness rests upon the *What for* before the *How*. *What for* is critical as it

conveys the intent, which is real: *What for* is the act's content and reality. *How* governs the form and ability to do: it is precise, steady, exact, attentive and orderly.
Mastering matter, plants or animals is not enough, **mastering the intent first is by far what matters**.

Never forget that these *presence* planes are embedded in your own. When you perform an act, you set these awareness degrees in motion, you focus onto their level. This is where your intent comes in.

Awareness is what this is all about.
Try and be in the lookout for every possible opportunity to act as a genuine human that comes within your reach. Most of the time, they come under the form of minute instants, so mundane that they are very easy to disregard. Each time however they are an opportunity for a choice of an awareness level where to act from.
When you do, you may feel a relationship build up, something happening between the stone, the tree, the animals, the humans and you. A new understanding, an accord, a vibrational connection manifests.
A joy.
Then, you know you are at the right place.

The fourth presence degree: the manifested human nature [xx]

Why are we humans?

Yes, what is our purpose in this world, our raison d'être?

The human *presence* degree is two-levelled: both manifested, as a *physical,* ordinary human being[1], and non-manifested, the *real* (non-physical) human, freed from time and space, whose *presence* is of all eternity [2].

This dual-level *presence* (*Jasmani-Rohani*) may be understood in a very simple way: **we, humans, are apprentices.** As manifested beings, we learn how to act *in awareness* with and in relatively rudimentary fields, the "manifested" ones, before

---

[1] The organic *level of presence*, where perception depends on an organ.

[2] The *Rohani* nature cf. on page 150

we evolve into a non-manifested *presence* state and act in all awareness at a subtler, therefore more active level [1].

We all are apprentices in active awareness, this is our purpose.

The higher the awareness degree, the more inclusive, consequent and active it is, the more what happens within it has an effect in the unified field of the *One-Awareness*. The wider the awareness degree, the more it acts within the essence of beings. The effects are indeed very powerful and vast.

Now our training makes complete sense: until we understand or master the effects of our *presence* within the fields we can access, our successive lives repeat within the realm of the manifested human, (*Jasmani*). Until the training bears fruits, until we clear our *presence* of all that clutters it and retains it at its current state, we will experience our current and future lives at this very same awareness degree[2]. So that we keep learning and eventually grow in awareness.

---

[1] *"Those who sow in winter reap in summer"* (the Gospel of Philip -7)

[2] Or the one we will be at when we die.

Here is the meaning and purpose of our presence in the world: **we are here to carry on with our apprenticeship in active awareness,** to become complete.

Now, what are these "tools and materials" we must learn to master? Quite simply, they are the four *presence* fields we can access, the constituents of "our" reality: the mineral, vegetal, animal and human planes.

Human beings are provided with all the qualities of the underlying *presence* planes. Because we are provided with these forces, we can know them, understand and use them. If this were not the case, we would not perceive them or know what to do with them.

Thus, just like the mineral plane, "ordinary" human beings are endowed with a deep sense of being, a purposeful self. Like the vegetal plane, they are endowed with sensations, like animals, they experience emotions and courage.

In addition, we humans are endowed with a quality that absolutely distinguishes us from the underlying levels, a perfect match to our own purpose: **we are aware of consciousness, we are awareness aware.**

And that precisely enables us to fulfil our raison d'être: to work in active awareness.

We have the capacity to distance from ourselves, to connect to what cannot be perceived within us, to what cannot be spoken of. We have this innate connection with the world of Spirit, including the *Rohani* level[1]. We can *act in awareness*, which gradually takes us to higher *presence* degrees.

Human beings, whatever their consciousness state, whatever happens to them, wherever they

---

[1] Here a word of caution may be advised: each awareness degree whether mineral, vegetal, animal or ordinary human, extends into its own spiritual realms, astral levels, which ought not to be confused with the *Rohani*. These can be reached by NDE or appropriate methods which can only take us to the spirited side of our current *presence* level. Confusing them with "heaven" is misleading and may even lock us down within subordinate paradises. After death, many keep on roaming these astral fields, some not having even noticed they are deceased. This is being hooked in the suburbs of matter, possibly because of a far too great attachment to it. Dead or alive, what we access depends on our own awareness state. Real spirituality takes us far beyond these spheres, it is a longer journey into wider and wider awareness degrees.

are, whatever their life circumstances, always keep the possibility to *become aware*, to be silent and interrogate.

Henceforth, we open in ourselves an access to the Real world of Spirit and begin with our apprenticeship. Would we choose not to, we would keep on playing in the *re-creation ground*, unaware of why we are here.

Until we get sated with the experience and interrogate.

Our "creation" power

At the core of our apprenticeship, we learn how to master our **"creation" power**. Through awareness, human beings greatly differ from the other manifested planes: we are given the possibility to choose the awareness degree wherefrom to shape and organise the world. At any time, we may change for one that is different from our usual ones and, thus, define another reality. Hence, human beings are "realities" makers[1].

The effects and manifestations of what we "create" directly derive from our *presence* degree[2],
wherefrom our intent originates.
It is all there.

In order to begin with our apprenticeship, we have to acknowledge and then understand how our awareness degree, our *presence,* defines the events, the circumstances, the "building blocks" of our reality. What *comes* and happens to us, all pre-exists as potentialities in awareness, which our intentions call forth and actualise.

Animals can roam the world, but merely a given world. Their environment is predetermined, as the one of plants and of minerals even more so. Animals, plants, stones are contingent to

---

[1] We do not *create* what seems to be the reality, we *make it appear*, through the interplay of intent, cause and effect, as a « chosen » slice within the immensity of all potentials, which is *present* in all eternity.

[2] Whether collectively or individually. Here we have a clue of the impact of mass media and "social" networks, on how they contribute and shape a collective awareness field.

circumstances while, as human beings, we "create" them. We are endowed with choice, the choice to shape this world, to evolve in awareness and create our reality in the direction we would rather experience. Provided we understand how it works and tidy up the mess in what agitates us.

To make it plain and simple, understand that, if we conceive our reality out of a material *presence*, it will be ruled by materialistic and egoistic urges and tensions, stubbornness, helplessness, insecurity and lack; if we conceive it from a vegetal awareness degree, it will be filled with judgments, craving desires and competitive drives; if we conceive it from an animal awareness plane, it will be filled with emotions, violence, predation and sexual urges.
And the world we live in begins to take shape.

We may see our rather long[1] human history as a slow, painful, arduous process of "evolution" in awareness, and who we collectively are shows the immense variety of awareness degrees we have been sharing for all times.

---

[1] Or short, depending on the perspective.

It is useful to comprehend that this "evolution" is Creation seen from our perspective, where time and space take place. **It tells our story, not Reality.** It tells how gradually we rise in awareness within the perspective of time. It tells how we amble within a gigantic variety of awareness degrees in the *One-awareness,* experiencing realities we may not be totally satisfied with, just because we are unaware of our purpose and tools as human beings.

Nonetheless, this creation power is but an illusion.

We *create* nothing.
More than a power to create, this is more a **power to re-create**, in every sense of it. We bring forth and actualise bits of reality that are pre-existent within the field of *One-Awareness*, what All is[1].
The absolute and vertiginous miracle of *Life* is this ability given to beings to do, to things and circumstances to appear, so that they interact and

---

[1] Wheeler proposed the idea that the universe and consciousness are deeply interconnected. One of his famous phrases is: **"It from bit :** *all physical things ("it") in the universe are fundamentally derived from information ("bit").* He suggested that the universe might be more like a giant information processing system, where consciousness plays a crucial role in shaping reality.

consequently to make it possible for the Source to experience All-Love within Itself.

The "creative" power of humans is solely the capability they are endowed with to actualise, **according to their awareness state**, the Reality "slice" they will experience.
Their *presence* plane determines the constituents of their reality, the reality they will experience, whether they are aware of it or not[1].

This may well be one of the most potent laws of Creation.

Awareness is like a shopping mall, with a multitude of floors. There is the one of play and the one of fear, the ones of power, ignorance and gift, the one of desires, the one of wealth and lack, the ones of detachment, of separateness, performance, adventure, the one of joy, bliss and gratitude, and countless others that mix them all with one another. Your own *presence* plane is the floor where you stand in the mall. The one that determines your world, the circumstances that you live and which your acts impact. When you give form to an intent, a thought or an act, you walk

---

[1] Cf. on page 188

around and shop *at a given floor.* If you genuinely wish for another reality, changing your modes of action or even intent will not suffice, they all come from the same floor. You have to change floor, to choose another awareness plane [1].

What is usually named *freewill*, is our ability to roam within a floor in the mall. The real freedom is to wander between floors, to let go of the *I.*

Then, freewill no longer *takes place,* in every sense of it.

From the *presence* degree which they actualise in their intents, and which materialises in their thoughts, acts and circumstances, humans determine the part of Reality which they experience.

Here you may understand the meaning, importance and reality of your apprenticeship.

---

[1] Going down in awareness is very easy, escalators that lead to the levels below are countless. In order to go up, one needs to pay attention. *Letting go,* the ability to detach from all what is at our floor, is the elevator that takes us to the upper levels.

This capability is precisely the one that distinguishes humans from all other levels of awareness within the manifested world, within the world of form.

There it is easy to comprehend that, from the combination of awareness states that occupy yourself, you "choose" to experience a world that is inspired (or even dominated) by matter, vegetal, animal or ordinary humans. Or by a mixture of all of that.

You may, just as well, choose a world that is inspired by the real human being in you, the Anthropos.

All these worlds and so many others co-exist. Here, now[1].

---

[1] Discrepancies between awareness degrees, or even reality conflicts happen all the time. Most of the time, we speak to one another but do not *comprehend* one another, the realities are disjoint, they do not match. We do not see the world the same way, as they actually *are* different. The only solution is *no conflict*, full acceptance, comprehension and forgiveness which bring us into a wider awareness degree. Even more so when the most rudimentary levels resort to violence, be it intentional, verbal or physical, which may drag the other down to this very level. One has/is lost when one responds to violence with violence. This helps understand

This capability is immense and perfectly operative, even though very few of us are truly aware of it. Like actors mesmerised by their dummy universe, most of us perceive this apparent world as the only "objective" reality, the tangible reality of artefacts. Their *presence* state does not enable them to open to the possibility of other realities, not to mention to choose among them.

If you can perceive how tragic it is for an actor to be locked in his role, to keep on wearing wig, props and disguise whilst shopping and walking the street, you may understand how vain most of our preoccupations and acts are in this world. Everything we are attached to is illusion.

Our dual polarity

As intermediaries between the manifested and non-manifested realms, humans have a dual polarity:

---

what Christ said: *If someone slaps you on one cheek, offer the other cheek also.*

- A "vertical" polarity[1] between *presence* degrees: they are at the same time manifested beings acting in this world in a physical body (the *Jasmani* human), and non-manifested beings acting only in awareness, in "spirit" (the *Rohani* human, Anthropos, the fifth *presence* degree).
- An "horizontal" polarity which corresponds to the masculine/feminine distinction which is impossible not to address.

At first, we ought to pay tribute to the magnificent ability of human beings to live their lives elongated between the unmeasurable and the derisory, to the vast, gigantic, strange "vertical" breadth of our human experience: we, humans, are stretched to the max between the immensity of That which touches us and extends wholly beyond us and our daily lives amid our worries, bills and chores. Between limitless Heaven and confined Earth that carries and nourishes us, between what irresistibly aspires us and what forcefully holds us, at the heart of those dimensions that contain and overwhelm us all the same. It is no wonder that most of us

---

[1] One understands that the concept of verticality, upper and below, is purely symbolic, it is just here to help discern and comprehend. It could be before/after just as well.

cannot stand the stretch and would rather live in a more restrained and comprehensible reality.

The incomprehensible miracle is that That which has no form and cannot be spoken of may be verged upon and "divined" in this world. Sheer admiration mixed with awe and gratitude is the only possible state, the sole solution, the only trace that remains.

Through your apprenticeship, you tend to unite these two polarities, masculine/feminine, non-manifested/manifested. You gradually clear from the illusion of separateness and join **Reality, a world where you experience oneness and individuation all at once**, where the qualities of the Source express with no hindrance whatsoever: nourishment and growth, protection and care, satisfaction of every need for all, work and activity, rhythm and order, respect of the universal laws.

The union of man and woman.

"This is how it is with those united in marriage.
The mystery that unites two beings is great.
Without it, the world would not exist.
What gives substance to the world is Anthropos.

What gives substance to Anthropos
Is an enduring and lasting relation [gamos]
Seek the experience of the pure embrace
[koinonia].
It has great power.
Contemplate the Presence in this impermanent
body.
Some of the unclean spirits are masculine, other
are feminine.
The masculine ones unite with
souls who inhabit a female form.
The feminine ones unite with
souls who inhabit a male form.
None can be free with respect to these forms unless
they receive
a power which is both masculine and feminine" [xxi]

We ought to tell and understand the masculine/feminine relationship in its profoundness, the utterly complementary roles at the highest level of Creation of the *Father*-vibration and the *Mother*-vibration, in perfect parity within the order of Creation.

The inseparable union of the *Intent to Be* (the content), the "masculine" inspirer-creator impulse with the *Sense of Being* (the vessel), the creator "feminine" form- creator impulse, is the indescribable manifestation of the *One-Awareness*, that is all there is[1].

This is where the **real Trinity** expresses itself in all its might and infinite beauty: the inaccessible unity of the Source, that is mighty to the infinite within Nil with neither form nor name and, <u>at the same time</u> (!), total *I Am-ness* in its comprehensive and dual expression, the intertwined *Intent to Be and Sense of Being*[2].

Then God said, "Let Us make man in Our image, after Our likeness"[xxii]

The masculine/feminine intertwined parity is Reality.

Conversely, it must be said that the one-sided, strained and excessive focus on the masculine in our world, coming together with the unrecognised, belittled, even negated or subservient perception

---

[1] To use here the masculine/feminine genders is a misnomer that enables us to understand the interweaving complementarity of the two creator-impulses which we are an expression of at the *Jasmani* level. Similarly with the words "father" and "mother" which used to be told by others who precisely knew what they were talking about.

[2] See on page 167

of the feminine, creates a world of delusion, of unbalance and lack, a world that is orphan, fake and vain. A world that drifts into nothingness. The cultures, customs or rituals, including the religious ones, that reduce the woman's freedom or status, that harm her physical, social, affective or emotional integrity must be denounced as practices that have no Reality within the *One-Awareness* whatsoever.

On the contrary, the perfect masculine/feminine balance, which stands beyond fears, rituals and creeds, ought to be acknowledged, explored, understood and manifested. Otherwise, we entrust our destiny to a sort of semi-god that we have fabricated, an idol made of our limits and fantasies, and we maintain our reality in illusory or even perverted awareness planes.

The Masculine tells what brings forth the intent, the impetus, the pre-conception of what is to come. This intent is operative, it sets the **content** of what happens, it **infuses** Creation which would not be without it.

The Feminine tells what gives form to what is conceived in spirit. It is all what protects, comforts, heals, nourishes. This nature is operative, it is the intent **vessel**, it carries, surrounds, nourishes and protects content, it gives shape to what happens, it **contains** Creation which would not be without it.

The masculine/feminine unity, Intent and Sense of Being **is what is.** In all eternity.

One does not go without the other, otherwise there would be no creation. The genders we experience are but the expression within this manifested plane, of the most fundamental Reality, the dual reality at the core of *I Am-ness.*

To conceive is <u>both and at the same time</u>, to express intent/content as well as to give shape/vessel to what is about to be.

What pulls man and woman towards each other, this inclination, this attraction at the deepest of ourselves, **is indispensable to our realisation at the human *presence* degree** [xxiii].

There is something truly extraordinary, profoundly sacred in the necessity, the inevitability of this union that is inseparable from love. Man and Woman, one does not go without the other, or more precisely, one goes nowhere without the other, except into a world of delusion, unreality and figments, a world of untruth.

«*We cannot insist enough on the fact that you will not discover the Truth about your existence until you have fully understood and sought to implement in your daily lives, your homes and your workplaces, your full understanding of the true meaning of "man" and "woman".* »[xxiv]

In the act of love, when the joint senses of being are clear from the grip of the lower planes, from the desires and egos, if man and woman are not in tension towards one another but immersed in a common awareness, in a state beyond their will or desire, then they can open to the *presence* of the *real* human being (*Rohani*). When the union is realised at this level, it bears real bliss. The sheer power of the **energy-awareness** that expresses at this point gives us a brief glimpse of what we can experience at this *presence* degree.

"The greatest spiritual reality between a man and a woman reveals itself when they can be together, naked and at peace, in a state of mutual reverence, in soul, spirit, heart and body. In such a spirituality state, all they feel from the other is love and respect for the other's well-being. From such a state of love and tender and compassionate care, rises a union

of a rapturous magnitude that few on Earth have experienced"[xxv]

For the time being and for quite a few of us, the approach, understanding and practice of the sexual act manifest an awareness that is largely encumbered by the animal or even material *presence* planes: through frenetic or even compulsive practices, jumbled with images, desires, fantasies if not accessories, they give free rein to their instincts, when it is not a matter of maintaining an ascendancy, a subjection on the partner, or worse when it is a matter of possession or even abuse.

These behaviours totally misconstrue the scope of the act of love, its very place in Creation, most often understood as the sole act of reproduction and pleasure.

"The bridal chamber
is not for animals nor for the slaves,
nor for the impure;
it is for beings who are free, simple and silent."[xxvi]

While the nature and intent of the act of love manifest the partners' *presence* degree, it is also true that, whatever the experience we choose to live, it is legitimate in regard of social norms, provided that it comes from a choice in *awareness*, that is voluntary <u>and</u> unconstrained between partners. We do have the freedom to choose the world experience we decide to make.

It is important however to be aware of the forces at work when we make our choices and, more importantly, to comprehend that the *presence* plane which they manifest, determines what comes to us.

Even more so if, in the course of this act, we remain at the physical and manifested planes. In that case the experience we live reinforces even more the grip of these forces onto our own sense of being [1]. **To the point of defining what the meaning of life is for us.**

Conversely, through an act of love in *presence*, our world experience may gradually evolve in awareness, become more human with more attention to the other, more compassion and patience, less separateness and judgment, more benevolence, respect, love, listening and taking the other into account in the fullness of his/her being.

---

[1] The grip of the lower degrees of awareness is substantially reinforced by the images, practices and lifestyles conveyed by the media, social networks and the *entertainment* industry.

In this state that nears the *real* human being (the *Rohani* plane), the partners accept each other in every dimension, and express the fullness of the human relationship. One for the other, they are at the same time man, husband, brother, boyfriend and father, woman, wife, sister, girlfriend and mother. Through this unconditional and selfless love, all these relationships express in their reality. It results in a fathomless tranquillity, a peace that verges on bliss.

Furthermore, the union of the *presence* fields deeply and durably imprints on each other's sense of being. Thus, the man or the woman may feel fulfilled, drained or even soiled according to what *occupies* their partner.

The integration of our human duality in love is an act that is immensely powerful. **It is through the act of love that all happens.**
On the one hand, it defines the reality plane where the partners meet, just like a switch that directs and fastens them into either a subtler degree, closer to the *One-Awareness* (the All-Love), or into subordinate planes (egotistic, separated realities). On the other hand, it is the focal point for the *presence* of a being to come. As a matter of fact, through this very act, we, humans, open an access into this world for an individuated *presence* that is

called forth to have yet another experience within the human plane. The joint partners' awareness field at the very moment of conception precisely resonates with that of the corresponding soul. This is nearly like an invitation.

Thus, what occupies us during the act of love, whether the man as a channel or the woman as a vessel, determines the initial *presence* plane of the being to come. This is not as a causal relationship, rather a matter of passage and resonance. Whatever the child's nature, whatever his/her *presence*, the parents may rejoice themselves at having enabled this awareness frequency to come into the world, what it longed for above anything else. Each conception manifests a life experience that needs to be lived.

Thus, parents and children are partners in a joint experience, each being in this world to continue with his/her own apprenticeship as a manifested human *presence*.

Together, they rise in awareness by combining experiences and mutual enrichment of what they are, learning from their children as much as from their parents. This is a very operative, powerful and profound partnership which, while we are at it, we ought to try and bring to completion. Education and awareness awakening is done by the parents and the child at the same time. Whoever has *raised* children, knows how powerfully they transform who we are, how much we learn from them about ourselves, how much we evolve thanks to them, provided that mutual listening and respect form between generations, so that each may rise in awareness at his/her own pace.

The good news is that this "rise in awareness" (this awakening) goes across generations: when children evolve in *presence,* they make their parents, grandparents as well as ancestors benefit from it[1]. Similarly, when parents evolve in awareness, it is beneficial to their children and descendants. This mutual awareness sharing acts as a proposal, an opening to a vaster degree and it is up to each of us to take the step, to let oneself be touched, so that it starts manifesting in our lives.

---

[1] Provided they keep connected with them in awareness. Hence perhaps the importance of worshipping the ancestors in several cultures and religions. We may just as well sense the extent to which the soul or *presence* of each or our ancestors (whatever their phase in life) is directly concerned with how we conduct our own existence at our level. This permanent and eternal connection/unity between « generations » is a continuous and active reality in the field of universal *presence.*

Hence, all of us participate in an immense *"presence* tide"*, rocked by awareness flow and ebb according to how we live, according to the *presence* fields we actualise through our intents and our acts, which is limited by neither time nor generations. On a closer look, this "solidarity" [xxvii] that is real within the fabric of filiations and relationships, is yet another cause for marvelling at our being *alive*.

The illumination

Illumination is the vertical integration of our being. It manifests a direct and open continuity between this world and the *Rohani*/Anthropos *presence* degree.

It tells the ability of human beings to let themselves be aspired by and become transparent to upper/wider Reality states. It tells the ability to live beyond our ego, to let this story we constantly tell us about ourselves all our lives long, evaporate. It tells the ability to clear ourselves from the imprints that shroud our perception of Reality to live the fullness of what Is.

Illumination is the end of the delusion of separateness. It is the access to the complete, real or accomplished human being, the integration of our *Rohani* awareness state.

Thus we "resurrect" in our lifetime and access this state where *being* is out of time and lives eternally.

This unity is completeness of the human being in his dual nature, manifested and non-manifested, physical and spiritual. It expresses through a constant feeling of grace, of bliss and wonder. An experience that is at the same time happiness and suffering, joy and pain as the opposite are reunited.

In the same way as sensations bridge the vegetal and animal planes, in the same way as emotions link the animal and human planes, likewise bliss is a passage marker between the ordinary and real human being.

To look for illumination, to desire it, to think of it even, is an oxymoron, a contradiction in terms. Illumination is neither searched, found nor reached. It is an awareness state that reveals itself and is lived by itself. It is a silence, a permanent and marvelling recognition of divine awareness, everywhere and in all.

That is all there is.

The fifth *presence* degree: the real human nature [xxviii]

Here begin the non-manifested realms of Creation, a world of order, bliss, grace and glory. Here all is at its place and works appropriately.

From this awareness plane onwards, beings are but awareness vibrations at frequencies that are high enough not to materialise. Welcome to the world of Spirit. A world of individuated though not separated beings, a world that is cleared from tangible form. A world of *presences* that are perceived just like variations of intents, fragrances, sounds or colours.

A universe of perceptions, of vibrations which are so subtle and refined that the senses are intensified, the spectrum of what is perceptible is opened and magnified. Each sense's *function* is active, but it no longer needs organs, or material supports to express itself. The Real Human being is complete. The amplitude at which he/she hears, sees, touches, smells, tastes, perceives, senses, feels, reaches levels one cannot possibly comprehend[1].

Thus, the *Rohani presence* degree is **filled with bliss and joy**. It vibrates within the power of rapture, this state which, at our current plane, we intermittently know, as if touched by a fragrance that reminds us of who we are and the direction of Home, of the Kingdom.

At this stage, the beauty of what Is can only translate into wonder and peace as well as a limitless and endless gratitude. The being experiences Love in its fullness. Love in bliss and joy, that is penetrating as a fragrance of the Source.
At this level of refined subtlety, time does not exist. All is, instantaneously, in all eternity.

At the *Rohani presence* degree, we join a world where separateness no longer takes place. Here we are one with the *One-Presence* **and** individuated all at once. In this state, whatever enters our consciousness (when we think of

---

[1] Yet it is possible to touch, smell, taste, hear a colour (one speaks of warm/cold colours), thoughts we perceive may be perfumed or foul.

someone or something), one becomes it[1]. Instantaneously. In the exact same way as perfumes, colours and sounds merge.

Therefore, beings who come close to this state in this world, may feel what the other feels, know what the other thinks. They sense the intent. They comprehend the other to the point of knowing precisely what he or she is about to say before they do so.

With a deep feeling of evidence, of something that goes by itself. A sensation of intense comprehension and non-differentiation.

At this awareness plane, all needs are perfectly met, they evaporate because the presence is filled, realised. This awareness degree is clear of the ego urges that generate lack, separation and illusion[2].

"It is impossible for anyone to see the everlasting reality and not become like it.

---

[1] In this awareness degree, to think is to act. Hence the importance for us, physical human beings, to learn how to be conscious of our thoughts.

[2] Cf. page 242

The Truth is not realised like truth in the world.
Those who see the sun do not become the sun.
Those who see the sky, the earth, or anything that
exists, do not become what they see.
But when you see something in this other space,
you become it.
If you know the Breath, you are the Breath.
If you know the Christ, you become the Christ.
If you see the Father, you are the Father.
In this Temple-Space, you become all things,
and you see yourself no more.
And in that All-Other, you become all things and
never cease to be yourself." [xxix]

The real human bathes in Primeval Presence, he vibrates therein with no limit or hindrance. He, therefore, intensely emits **Love and Respect**. This is what he feels for everything within the awareness fields he accesses, whatever it is.

The Real human, the *Rohani* being, has all the manifested *presence* degrees within her. They are perfectly known to her and in order within her. Thus, her *presence* field comprehends what we are and what we are living.

In the very same way as the physical human being tends to the manifested *presence* planes, the Real human, who perceives them all, is attentive to what we are *in awareness*, helps us express our genuinely human qualities in this world.

Again, can you understand the importance of living *in awareness?* This is the only way to let yourself be touched by That within you, that which wants to inspire and guide you. From then on, the Real human *presence*, may become a continuous source of inspiration for you.

The channel exists as we are endowed with awareness, we can talk about it. Through that means it goes.

Therefore, let the fragrance of this *presence* infuse within you. It tells you, once your desires and wills are impregnated with the Source and cleared from what you believe you are, how all the qualities of the *One-Awareness* may appear to you, to which this awareness state accesses fully: it speaks of abundance, joy, bliss, love and peace, equilibrium and order; it speaks of one-awareness with the other, of activity and rhythm; of gift that is innate because unwilled. A world in continuous conversation with the divine.

This is Reality at the *Rohani* awareness degree.

Its purpose is **to guide, to awaken, to teach**.

Now is the proper time to speak of Christ, no other moment would be more appropriate.

This man came to show us who we are, beings of *presence*, all at once humans facing the Earth and spirits facing the Origin.

Christ, as we may *re-cognise*[1] him, is both Real Human (or human accomplished) and above all, the manifestation of a dual nature at an even subtler and more powerful degree.

Christ is a promise at its highest: an ordinary man and Real human while in this world, the time of his life in Palestine (*Jasmani and Rohani*), he is at the same time Christ in all eternity, the highest possible nature in the Order of Creation, the *Rabbani presence* plane[2], a dimension he accessed at the "end of his life" on Earth.

While living on Earth, he constantly defined himself as the *Son of Man*, acknowledging his nature as a complete Human, the *Jasmani/Rohani presence*. He is now and for all times a *Rabbani presence*.

"I am the Way and the Truth and the Life".

---

[1] To invite in us, to be with, as at subtle levels of *presence,* to think of is to be.

[2] See on page 162

When he experienced this world, he fully completed his role as a *Rohani* being: to guide, to awaken, to teach [1].

He did not come to tell us of a God outside of us. He came to reveal the "good news": the realm of the true Human and the ability given to us, human beings, to generate a "reality" from awareness, from the active power of *Presence* and of Love.
He came to tell us about the Source and Reality.
The Source manifested as Father Intent to Be and Mother Sense of Being.
Our reality as beings of *presence*, created and creators who participate in the manifestation of the Source.

"For the child of true Humanity exists within you. Follow it! Those who search for it will find it. Go then, preach the good news about the Realm."[xxx]

The beauty of the coming of Yeshua[2] in this world, the promise and power of his message dwell within his life, his teachings and miracles of course, but even more, within his active *presence* among us.

---

[1] Mary Magdalena called him the *Teacher*.
[2] His Jewish name. Jesus is the Greek transcription.

Beyond parables and words, he came to deliver a simple message to us:

The entire universe, Creation in its entirety is begotten by the Origin. All beings are parts of *awareness*, we all are, everything is, a minute fraction of *Love-Awareness* that is the everlasting expression of the Source. As humans, we are creators at and from our own *presence* level, we make a given aspect of Reality happen **and we can change it,** just as well, within our awareness field. When opening our *presence* to Reality, we may be given the possibility to discover and live the Kingdom. We all can realise precisely this and are all precisely called to realise this. This is our purpose.

The union between the Father, "content/ inspiration" creator-impulse (*Intent to Be*) and the Mother, "form/vessel" creator-impulse (*Sense of Being*) continues for all eternity. This is the Marvel of Marvels, the reality of Creation within, with and for *Love-Awareness*.

Maybe now is the time for us to comprehend it again.

"Do not let my work be in vain for a second time. As you read these pages, search, meditate and pray to receive inspiration. You will come to feel the

answer from the Father and if you listen attentively each day, you will hear the Father's voice. This voice is with you for all eternity. Dismount the barriers created by will and ego. Open yourself to receive strength, power, inspiration and love directly from the Father's Love Awareness." [xxxi]

The sixth *presence* degree: the nature of Gift [xxxii]

From here on, words are somewhat flimsy, just let yourself be surrounded with silence, be guided and let the words come, those that can be written and those that cannot.

How can one possibly describe with forms, that which is beyond them all, an unthinkable perfection?

Open your mind even more. Here the essential reads between words. Like silence between the clock strikes.

There, you might be given to feel through the finest sensation how this *presence* degree is even vaster, more complete, more embracing and closer to the Source. It is the **ultimate expression of the Gift. Compassion at its purest state, with no hindrance nor compromise** [xxxiii].

Here, there only is Gift and nothing else. Gift and forgiveness as a nature of bliss. A few mystics seem to have had a taste of it, to have vibrated at this *presence* degree.

This is the place wherefrom all prayers are answered, as soon as they are asked. All of them.

This *presence* state is the Compassionate Heart, the ultimate non-judgment, non-separateness. At this level, *Presence* neither holds nor rejects nor condemns. This is the precise opposite to a stern, haughty and punishing divine, the sacrifice demander which we have been taught for ages by a few religions.

In such a high and subtle *presence* state, whoever, wherever, whenever, for whatever reason would deserve to be judged, finds here immediate absolution. Every being is understood, accepted and forgiven. There is neither good nor harm done or inflicted, neither victim nor tormentor, we are at the Heart of Forgiveness. Moreover, forgiveness has no reason to be as there is no fault nor guilt. There only is compassion.

This does not mean that the immutable universal laws of Creation do not apply, no one can evade, erase or deviate from them, most of all the law of cause and effect. This implies that every being can only experience the consequences of his/her acts[1]. But, at this *presence* degree, whatever their deeds, all beings are known and acknowledged as being part of the *One-Awareness*. They are loved and supported for who they are, beings who participate in Creation, bearers of the Source essence.

Whatever the path they must follow in the infinite of times.

This awareness degree is the profound and perpetual loving *Presence,* which every of us may feel, whatever our life circumstances may be, provided we let this fragrance of the Source permeate our own confinements and separations. Provided we let it guide and inspire us.

---

[1] The cause/effect *separation* is specific to our manifested world where space and time apply. In the unmanifested one, it does not exist as cause and effect are one. There is no separation, only act/intent, hence cause and effect merge in the experience. Cf. page 208.

At this vibrational level, in this state, the totality of all beings reunites, beknown and absolved. Every being, everything is loved in its singularity, shared, understood, integrated.

This is the *presence* degree where **Creation rejoices in grace**. At this stage, Creation is a pure, immense, unthinkable and sublime embrace. The awesome feeling of Oneness in the multitude of its diversity, loved, acknowledged, respected.

We will soon tell the seventh heaven, but the sixth already is something!

Hence in the ultimate order of Creation, the *One-Presence*, the primeval Mother, unfolds all awareness fields and degrees by having them pass through this condition of absolute Gift, the mark, the filigree of the divine in all creatures: all that exists, all that is created is touched by the *Presence* of Gift, all is worthy of Compassion. This is like a dye, an immersion, an imprint within each of us, whether humans, animals, plants or things. All is worthy of the Gift, of receiving the Gift. Every *presence* degree is comprised in that state.

To this point of forgiveness, guilt is naught.

This is neither an abstraction nor a concept. Contrarywise, as you read this, let yourself be touched by a profound sense of reality that grows within, immensely profound and unreachable to your mind but which your heart may recognise.

There, it rejoices and weeps in gratefulness.

The seventh presence degree: The nature of Love [xxxiv]

"Love is perfect stillness and the greatest excitement and most profound act and the word almost as complete as His name." [xxxv]

The *Intent* at the origin of all beings and things is All-Love, perfect and unmeasurable Love. The All-Love that is supremely intelligent and mighty. The All-Love that is comforter, protector, nurturer, healer, benevolent and dispenser of goodness.

There is and will always be **only That**. For ever.

Love beyond words and imagination.

This *presence* level is the ultimate *I Am-ness,* the most complete and comprehensive manifestation of the Source.

Beyond and at the deepest within, there is Nil, naught filled by the *Intent to be.*

This state is in unconceivable **Glory**. It is in eternal and absolute equilibrium within Divine *Presence,* the awareness of being in the entirety of what will ever exist.

And *Light is,* expressing unmeasurable love.

This state of Love *presence* is the climax of Creation, its beginning and its end, it contains it all in its *infinite and eternal completeness.*

The entire Creation is at this point.

All-One.

To be at this point of Love is to be in wholeness, in embrace of All. This is a state of absolute, peaceful equilibrium, far beyond selfless love, far beyond Agapè. This is a state of total transcendence where Be and Love fuse within each other, express each other, as perfect manifestation of the fusion of the primeval impulses.

This ultimate and primeval state is the Infinite Field of All in potentiality. It is the ultimate oneness of Creation in its wholeness, of all eternity. All is expressed, instantaneously, born from Nil. Creation as the primeval and unique expression of the Source.

Christ *is* at this *Presence* level [1], a nature that is primeval, ultimate and infinitely glorious.

The Mother of all beings and things. Here we are at the apex of the divine embrace: the Source comprehended and expressed by the whole Creation. Creation intended and enlivened by the Source.

"Whatever we have done or not done of the opportunities that were given to us when we were conceived (or of the lack of those), we are all fundamentally from the very same potential and same state of being. Each of us can progressively grow in awareness, to eventually reach the heights of Divine Awareness. Christ awareness. What

---

[1] As well as Muhammad s.a.w

makes the difference between beings in the instant is what this person gives of herself at this given moment, then the next, then the rest of the day, then the next." xxxvi

This *presence* degree bears, comprehends all the Creation orders that will develop to various degrees into all its awareness states, all that the living expresses.

A dazzling flash of expansion, of creative might and at the same time, nourishment, care, protection and satisfaction of needs. All in rhythm and order.

Here silence is a thundering music.

I Am-ness

The Marvel of marvels

The Source Is.

Intent to Be within Nil, that is silent, inaccessible, infinitely loving and eternally powerful, impossible to describe, impossible to join.

From this unconceivable Intent, *I Am-ness* is born under the form of a **dual *presence* vibration, which is and traverses all Creation, from its highest level down to its scantiest.** A dual vibration that is immensely active, with unspeakable power, an energy made of Intent and Awareness intertwined: *Dhat Allah* and *Sifat Allah* [1], the twin inseparable impulses mentioned at the beginning of this story.

- *Dhat Allah,* the **Divine Essence.** The "inner messenger", the divine *Power* that expresses and infuses the Intent. The power-impulse of expansion and conception. The spark that guides. The Source's *Intent to be* which spans across the whole universe and all worlds at the deepest of all creatures. It is infinite by

---

[1] Islam

nature as it knows no limit. An oh, so loving Intelligence! Some call it the Great Life Force, the Breath, the *Clarifier* or the *Enlightener*. The Christians name it the *Holy Spirit*, the Muslims the *Light of Muhammad*, the Jews *Ohr Mimalei Kol Olmin*. It manifests through our highest and most beautiful inspirations. The source of our enlightenments, it feeds our flashes of understanding and intuition. It is the absolute Content which enlivens all that is.

- *Sifat Allah,* the **Divine Nature**. The "outer messenger", the divine *Presence* that creates and enfolds all forms. The vessel-impulse that shapes, structures and carries. The Source's *Sense of being* which is and expresses all the universes, worlds and beings in an ultimate perfection. The matrix which contains all there is. It is eternal by nature as it knows no time. It is the absolute Vessel, the amniotic *Presence* of All, where every being or thing bathes in all times[1] . Love oh, so intelligent! which makes every form graceful, at the same

---

[1] *The Tao is called the Great Mother: empty yet inexhaustible, it gives birth to infinite worlds. It is always present within you. You can use it any way you want.* Dao De Jing (VI)

time operative, surprising and creative, which expresses the Reality's exactness and precision.

Dhat Allah and *Sifat Allah,* the Marvel of marvels. The dual Reality that expresses the Source, the Divine that Is all there is.

Mother-Presence, which is the fabric of Creation and *Father-Breath* that traverses and wrinkles it, to give birth to an infinite number of waves, of awareness vibrations that are created to share, realise and witness Creation.

I Am-ness ceaselessly traversed by waves of *Presence,* beings of Light-awareness, all at once bearers of the Origin Intent and witnesses-guardians of the precision and exactness of Creation, that are both active and present within all worlds, capable of taking any shape within every degree.

Angels.

Divine Essence and Divine Nature, one in labour for eternity, what we call the Living.
The inner and the outer, the twin expressions of Divine, the two ways of *comprehending* Reality, to be, to live as well as to witness it.

To serve.

Let us remember one thing: nothing of what we live, do or endure is for our own account.

Nothing
Again, nil.

All is done *on behalf of* That and *by* That. The ultimate awareness by which and within which all is. Because all comes from the *One-Awareness*, proceeds from it and returns to it. And if, while in an act, you let yourself be inspired by the Breath, then it becomes like the profound resonance of a bell that vibrates and ripples to the highest of Creation.

Our *we*, your/my *I* borrow from the *One-Awareness* to act and to feel, to experience Reality. All beings are *just* individuated sensations of *presence*, awareness folds by the trillions that are in charge of experiencing Reality. For ever.

We are and daily live the marvel of marvels.

The perfect, sublime, operative union of these twin impulses, of the dual nature of divine Reality is given to us to live every day. Ceaselessly and in the infinite of times. An unspeakable joy, a wonder within and without at the same time.

Nuptials.

This is where we are. This is what we live. This is what to be alive means.
What more can we say?
A single word suffices to tell and feel what all this is about.

Worship.

The rest is silence.

I Am-ness

Our five powers

At this stage of your path in wonder, pause for a while, observe and listen.
As often as possible.

Look at the sea, a landscape, a peak covered in snow, a painting from Vermeer, Gauguin, Turner or Hokusai, listen, yes, listen to the wind, the birds, a nocturne or a prelude from Chopin or Bach, a sonata from Mozart.
See the mother's eyes, the ploughman's, the sailor's and the nurse's.

Listen to the people passing by and the words they say.

We are ceaselessly witnesses of the human and of the world. All these big things and these scores of small ones, which never are as beautiful, never touch as much as when they are done for themselves, for the sake of life. Everything, every occurrence is an opportunity for this profound and selfless inspiration which is part of ourselves to break through when we let it happen.

Every being, every created thing has an exact place in creation. Ours, the one of every one of us is magnificent. We have been entrusted with mighty powers to tend to the visible world, to make it a humane reality.

A humanity.

We may experience the Living in two ways:
- Our usual one, the outside, *non-present* manner which makes us believe that we master the game or, at the opposite, that we suffer from events and circumstances upon which we can do little, if not totally random.
- Or the enlightened, inside and *present* manner, the inspired way where we let ourselves be surrogate creators **in proportion to how much we give of ourselves. In proportion to how far we forget about ourselves.**

Where, while doing so, we carry on with our apprenticeship in being, in divine awareness.

There are five powers that are accessible to us, that we are entrusted with:

- **The power of love.** Few of us can perceive, marvel at, even less use the immeasurable power of Love. How we usually experience love is a version of it that is somewhat simplified, cursory and tainted with affects and desires. Love in this world is like pasta or rice, we have it in all kinds of sauce, which is just fine as it comes in all kinds of flavour while, at a deeper and wider level, Love is the raison d'être of all. It is all the same the origin, the content, the state and the end of all Creation. When one places oneself at this level, one embraces all and knows that *ultimately, all is and is done in love.* All is at its place.

- **The power of *presence*.** It defines our reality, the *Love/I Am-ness* degree we move around in. How we live any circumstance, choices or decisions we make are only the crystallisation of a *presence*/awareness degree which we ignore most of the time. Generally speaking, presence or awareness is a vague hazy abstract, a diffuse concept tainted with moralism, philosophy or religiosity. Something in the realm of thought one does not precisely know what to do with. Yet awareness is precisely what Creation is made of, it is at the same time its source, its structure, and its substrate. **It goes exactly the same at our human level**: awareness is the source, the structure and substrate of what we give ourselves to live. Of the experience we want to make of ourselves.

- **The power of intent.** It precisely derives from awareness and defines the content of what we want to live. It is the backbone of the act; it provides the direction around which events and encounters organise like organs. This power creates a human link that is very deep, the one of innate trust (or mistrust). Once the intent is expressed, perceived and shared, there is no need for persuasion.

- **The power of form.** Nature is the song of form and the other way around. The form assesses contexts, circumstances, the nature of things and beings. The form outlines the act and enables us to interact between humans. It defines how things and beings are organised and arranged.

- **The power of resolution** which we daily use, is the tool with which to interact with the subordinate awareness degrees.

Willpower is not supposed to be used among humans.

When awareness gives rise to an intent, it opens the door to conception, next comes the act, which brings forth the form together with resolution and this whole process actualises the awareness level which the intent derives from. Once we understand this, we need nothing else. There the Living rushes into, with all its might and joy.

The act's very nature precisely depends on how we use these powers.
-   From which *presence/awareness* degree does it come from? Egotistic and self-oriented, or *loving*, selfless and universal, participating in the whole?
-   Which *intention* (*Dhat*), which level or ourselves does it express? How far does it leave space to service or inspiration?
-   Which *form* (*Sifat*) does it take? How far does it comprehend and accept the contexts, the equilibriums and natures in place?
-   Which *resolve*, courage, commitment (*Asma*) does it manifest?

Sometimes, yes sometimes, an act is truly beautiful, immense, however minute, or unnoticed it may be.

Here comes another piece of understanding: **the result (*Af'al*) does not belong to us.** It proceeds from the powers we borrowed and describes how coherently we have used them.

Here is an example to illustrate: in a true state of love, you have an acute, genuine and profound awareness of the "other", of his/her needs. This awareness will set events, encounters and circumstances in motion, which will "confirm" this reality in many different ways: various manifestations of the evidence, the urgency even, of the needs, blatant proofs of inadequacies or sufferings that will speak to you and touch you, indications of where you can act, what you can be. Your awareness field, your *presence* "constructs" the opportunity to act.

From then on, you generate an *intention* (an awareness impulse, which is a focused and dynamized energy) which bridges your sense of being with the opportunity to act. For instance, to heal people, to protect them, to comfort them, to educate them.

Therefrom, according to the circumstances that keep coming forth, you may decide on the *form* of your project, its goal[1]: to build a clinic, to become a pharmacy researcher, a nurse, a surgeon or doctor. You may as well decide to train mothers, children or elderlies to take care of their health in an autonomous way, with no other tool than your own talent and capacity to interact and relate with one another.

Completion will follow, the play with circumstances which demands persistence and resolve. Then you will be able to assess the coherence of your deeds by their *results* on people: how they are, how they feel, their state of mind. You may even be able to feel this result alive within you **before** seeing it actualise. You will know.

These powers are profoundly real. They are our "creator" tools and if you have tried them without getting the expected results (!), there is a reason for this: you just did not use them properly. It has nothing to do with their reality or efficiency.

---

[1] It is key to learn how to distinguish the intention from the goal. The intention comes from the inside and is personal, while the goal has a form, it shows in the outside and may/must be shared. The intention is an energy, it translates into a goal which, once achieved, keeps this energy within.

Can you feel how progressive these powers are? How they raise us into profound and *real* worlds that are subtler and subtler?

Do you perceive the different reality degrees they relate to? At the most tangible level, the reality of engaged and will-powered people, then the one of designers and organisers, then the visionary and inspired people driven by their intent that is more or less luminous or enlightened possibly, then the reality of beings of awareness and eventually the reality of beings of love.

All these beings are not necessarily different. They may just as well be the facets of the very same one manifesting different aspects of his/her reality.

The power of love

"People need to see and fully realise the intention, the purpose and the potential of love which is the very substance of their being." [xxxvii]

"The creature yearns for love. The creator loves."[xxxviii]

As we now know, love is inherent to the *Intent to Be*. It is by love and for love, under the unspeakable power of love that the primeval equilibrium of the *Intent to Be* broke through within Nil. Love is the impulse, the content and the purpose of creation all at once. It is its very "beginning" and "end".

Here, it is better to forget all about the pictures and interpretations we usually associate with love. Love which is spoken of here has very little in common with the one we may feel.

And yet.

While it has nothing to do with emotions, what we know of it makes it possible, at our human level, to experience what directly derives from the primeval, all-mighty, unconditional and absolute love.

Love is at the same time unstoppable impulse and profound contentment, movement and stillness; it is what grows and what is. It is what searches and what stays in peace; it is what is unconditional and what is specific. It is what burns and what soothes, what devours and what nourishes. It is at the same time immense joy and profound sadness, it contains and overwhelms, it is all at once the strongest sense of being and of being no longer, it is what makes us so fragile and so strong. It is this certitude that feels uncertain. It is what electrifies us and what magnetises us, what takes us to the furthest from ourselves and close to the most intimate of the other.

It is the vastness we feel as soon as we stop and delve into the instant. Which makes us speechless.

It is what is everywhere at home and what inhabits the world, what men and women have been singing since the dawn of times and which we will keep chanting for millenniums. It dwells at the heart of our biggest pains, our most intense sufferings. It is our greatest joy. It is what enfolds and soothes all our separations. It is what instantly heals and nourishes at every level of creation.

That which, by any way, cannot be contained.

To love, to live and to create are ultimately the very same and unique vibration, the same and sole impulse.

Love is at the heart of what we are and what enacts us. When we wonder about the infinitely small, about what vibrates at the deepest of our cells, about the void that inhabits us, this is love we come to. When we observe the cosmos, the space that is infinitely vast and distant, these countless galaxies that are moving away at dizzying speeds, this is love we contemplate: it is the song of the universe and the infinite substance of all what is. Contemplate the power hidden at the core of matter and you will see the might of love.

Now get back to the seven awareness levels, the seven *presence* planes which were mentioned above. Be enthralled again by the exquisite wonder of the interlaced impulses *Dhat Allah* and *Sifat Allah* which carry them, contain them, enliven and traverse them. All are expressions of love. There is only that. Each of these natures, each of these forces is a form of love.

Love that pulls and restrains, love that pushes and repels, love that assimilates and expands, love that multiplies, gives and nourishes, love that protects and fights, love that takes awareness, organises and acts.

This is simply astounding.

If you look at yourself, consider your family, partner, neighbours, friends and colleagues or these strangers across the road, you will see love, which every of us is made of and we all carry.

In all what we, humans, can do when we act, love or even hate, which are the two faces of the same token, the two sides of the same summit, the opposite expressions of the same reality - the Source - we see the unmeasurable power of love.

Love is operating: if we make the choice of acting from unconditional love, without leaning towards the other nor being in tension towards oneself, then we become miracle makers. Literally. This is as simple and immediate as that.
You may try whenever you want.

There are three jewels that I cherish: love, moderation, and humility.
With love, you will be able to be brave,
With moderation, you will be able to give to others,
With humility, you will be able to become a great leader.
To abandon love while seeking to be brave, or abandoning moderation while being benevolent, or abandoning humility while seeking to lead will only lead to greater trouble.
The loving warrior will be the winner, and if love is your defence, you will be secure.
Love is the Heaven's salvation.[xxxix]

To do, decide, think or want something out of love transcends everything. This is no philosophy nor creed, this is Reality which we may experience at any time, night and day. Here and now if we want.

The feedback is immediate. In the other's eyes, in the sensation that rushes inside, in the minute or vast peace that fills the instant. In the feelings people express, not knowing why.

In joy.

Love is your mightiest power, the most operating and precious one. Try it, use it and you will see how far it operates and transforms.

As much as it is an evidence, love is a choice.
As much as it is a storm, love demands attention.
Whatever the circumstances, you may always choose the power of love.

Pay attention to those who speak of love and respect at the same time. They are on their way to the real human, the *Rohani* degree. In the encounter of love and respect, a sort of quietness oozes, an inner tranquillity which makes you feel comfortable at home.

Love and respect begin with oneself. Are you still judging or are you fully accepting yourself? Do you have "weaknesses", shortcomings, flaws, lacks or, conversely, do you see yourself gifted, efficient, powerful? All these express an awareness of separateness, of non-acceptance of what is. If, on the other way round, you accept yourself as you are, if you see yourself alive within the world, with the fullness of who you are among and with others, then you enter an awareness of abundance, growth and joy. Everything becomes experience, everything is enrichment.

Only when you feel tranquil and happy within togetherness, in being among others, you may *realise* your human nature.

"When people are together, when harmony binds them all, they are fully aligned with the power of the One-Creator-Awareness." [xl]

These moments spent in the "we" tell us who we are and the full savour of humanity. A humanity that is on the move, in a constant equilibrium between what we believe we are and what we wish we could be, between where we go and whence we come. Each instant is this eternity, tensed between our polarities, as well as this joy of being who we are.

Just like children at play.

We are all utterly equivalent within an awesome diversity. We are a kaleidoscopic illusion where

Presence appears, shattered into tiny bits. **We are one**, this is Reality and if, when contemplating this, an emotion, a joy, a regret or a pain surges, welcome it, it tells you how much you are human and love the world. And if nothing comes, if nothing goes, it does not matter, other instants will follow, elsewhere, otherwise. Life is made of this.

Receive what the moment is made of, without thinking or wishing anything. There is no sweeter experience than being alive with others within the instant. Then we may feel the oneness that lives within us with all that is around. We may even have the surprise of finding us all beautiful. Yes, we are beautiful, whoever we are, when we are at peace with what we together are. It is like bathing in a water that is still, vast and clear, at the perfect temperature. We have no desire of getting out, we totally let ourselves go.

This, above all, is an exercise of peace and silence. With a little attention, it is possible to feel all the power that "we" express. All our respective paths, trajectories, life projects criss-cross in a living and colourful fabric that moves enlivened.

Us, one.

The power of *presence*

All is *presence.* One could stop there and have said it all.

Reality, the experience of life, is not a state that exists outside of oneself, things and circumstances that are external to us. Perception is an act of *presence.* It is a two-sided experience: we understand it as a "reception" of a world that we sense and consider as external, whilst it is **also and at the same time** an "emission" of a dynamic and changing *presence* field which we constantly project and actualise.

"You see but not radiate. Your eyes were not meant to see."[xli]

It is through this reflective experience that our *presence* field devises the components, the reality building blocks (events, people, circumstances, beings) which match its frequency and appear in our lives.

"The whole universe manifests the various vibration frequencies of awareness-energy particles. While these frequencies go up and down from a level to another, so do the physical and visible structures that manifest these various energy levels, in correspondence with the changes in mental and emotional states as well as appearances." [xlii]

When several beings simultaneously participate in an event or circumstance, **it is not the same for everybody!** It is lived by each participant in a distinct manner.

It is a frequent cause for misunderstanding to believe that what is perceived by one is identically experienced by the other. One takes one's own truth for THE truth, while each perceives according to his/her own *presence* field. This one will see an opportunity to rejoice, that other to sadden. This one will see an opportunity to fight and affirm himself, that other to admire and be thankful. People will smile at this one, the other will see problems. This one will want to leave, that other to stay... Our world is an astounding and mostly imperceptible superposition of intricated awareness fields which give birth to an awesome lot of different perceptions, intents and acts.

Anything "positive" that comes to us is a confirmation, a validation of our *presence* state. We are comforted, in the sense of comfortable as well as reassured. Anything "negative" that happens to us is a proposition for a change of *presence* state. It is a disagreeable experience, in the sense of dissonance and unpleasantness.

And the other way around is true as well! To think and act "positively" actualises a wider awareness degree, when negativity shrinks it.

You see how it works? It is all in the instant, in the being.

Our reality directly derives from our sense of being. When confused, it is a projection of our own confusion. When at peace, it expresses the peace within us.

If you observe what comes to you, you have a direct indication of where your *presence* field vibrates at this moment and which direction it takes.

Observe and listen.

There are things you see no longer or not yet, things you hear no longer or not yet, you no longer feel or not yet. Things you no longer want to touch or taste. All of this speaks of you, about the reality within you.

Of your share in Reality. Of your *presence*.

And all of this is on the move, with ups and downs, a rising tide. Alive.

Human.

Observe yourself: when you see, be aware of your sight. Listen to how you listen, smell how you smell. Put your consciousness behind the act, not within. Do not confuse yourself with what you do. **Be the awareness behind what you do**, it will soon become a habit, and it will be easier then to realise what enacts you.

Thence it becomes clear that, when we free our *presence* field from the layers that accumulate within it, when we grow in awareness, we alter our perception. We increasingly see, hear, feel, perceive things, beings and circumstances as the expressions of What Is. We merge in What Is and detach from our stories, desires and illusions.

The world literally changes.

In the other way round, when we feel the world is changing, it signals that we are living a movement in awareness, whatever the direction it takes. Just like a departing train: you do not feel the pull, but you see the platform moving backwards.

A *presence* field is a fabric, a substrate, a share of divine Awareness within which each of us "fabricates" his/her life. In return, our reactions, our responses to life circumstances modify and act upon our *presence* degree: they either reinforce it or make it evolve.

At any instant.
Every instant is an opportunity to live in awareness, to make the choice of movement or not. Life is precisely that: *presence* and movement. Within every instant we live at the core of impermanence, so dear to Buddhists, in equilibrium not so much between before and after but **between again and otherwise** rather.
Every instant is an occasion to be otherwise. To change *presence* degrees as we would clothes.

Hence, becoming aware of your *presence* degree is the most important step you may take in your life.

There you catch hold of your humanity.

This step, you may choose to take it whenever you like.
Why not now?

"You judge of your todays, and you expect from your tomorrows according to what you experienced in the past. Subsequently all the troubles of your yesterdays keep on reproducing in your life."[xliii]

In order to heal, change, evolve and modify the nature of circumstances that happen to you, you must act on your awareness level, not on your intentions, goals or actions. At these stages, it is already too late, things have been determined[1]. In order to heal, you must mend your creeds, the very substance at the origin of what you conceive, of your thoughts and intentions.
However, changing is not a matter of willpower. It suffices to be aware of what stirs and enacts you. The rest will come by itself. Willpower has nothing to do with *presence.* Only when you feel the possibility of a choice.

---

[1] If we get back to the shopping mall image, you may want a toy or a piece of clothing while roaming at the furniture floor, you will never find any. You must change floor.

"Your" *presence* (awareness, *I Am-ness*) is eternal, it is what you are of all times, it depends on neither your form nor incarnation. Your consciousness, the brain activity that generates and manages willpower, was born with you, it is impermanent and specific to this incarnation. You will keep nothing of it in the hereafter.

Be careful, though! You may want to change your consciousness state in order to make your fate lighter or progress, but such an intention may obstruct you at the level of egotistic concerns, turned towards your own benefit, taking care of your own fate.

It is vital to understand that willpower has nothing to do with this.

In order to grow in awareness, you do not have to want, you just have to be.

Willpower is merely a tool; intent is the hand that holds it and *presence* is the being that gives its direction.

Your *presence* field is somehow cluttered with the material, vegetal, animal, ordinary human planes, with all the response programs that come with them and compress your true nature. All these vibrations, these parasites are like a noise that covers the signal, they create a field that is more or less permeable to the *Presence* at the core of our beings, to the inspirations and illuminations of the Great Life Force.

The more it is permeable, the closer our manifested reality will be to our real human nature, a nature that is complete and free from the tensions, the imprints and stories, the defences and lacks that are all fabricated by our egos.

Therefrom comes our ability to be miracle makers. It appears when, by our *presence*, our intent or the mere fact that we direct our thoughts there, things seem to unravel and set themselves in motion and place.

Without the need for intervention.

For those who practice not-doing, everything will fall into place. [xliv]

One only works miracles for others. Life works them for our own sake.

At first, these states of peace and tranquillity are elusive and temporary, but the more one tries at them, the more one feels at ease and gets used to them like a second (or first) nature, the more the corresponding state of the world and how one experiences it, sets itself in place and holds up.

The power of intent, the content (*Dhat*)

Intent makes awareness perceptible. It actualises it. Each time we articulate an intent, we re-enact the Big Bang: we make something emerge out of nothing.

This is what intent is for: to generate a reality out of nothing, from a mere (!) awareness vibration. Intent focuses the awareness energy, puts it *in tension* until it is released in the act. Exactly as a capacitor that has been sufficiently charged suddenly discharges.

Every thought is a dynamized and focalised awareness form. It is endowed with a proper energy which "momentarily" stirs and tweaks the fabric of the *One-Awareness* we are immersed in. Thinking intently of someone or something instantaneously connects you to this person or thing, whether you are aware of it or not. On a subtle plane, you *join with* this person, and she can feel this link which strengthens or weakens her own energy, her own vibration, according to the nature of the intention which was carried by the thought. We join with things too and our intent creates a channel between them and our own *presence* state and if it lets itself be occupied by the thing *presence* field, it generates a bond, a craving for this thing.

As we can see, intent is an energetic channel, it is awareness polarised. If you practice archery, darts, golf or basketball, you already know this power. You know this moment when, having *intently* interiorised the target, you totally let the movement go, fully trusting that your body, guided by your intent, will perform the proper gesture. So, we daily have the proof, in these circumstances or others, that our ability to generate an intent determines the quality of what follows.

Intent is what creates the **content** of what you embark on. Whatever it is. Would it be a drawing, a thing, an enterprise, a journey. Intent is what matters; it designs the trajectory of what follows. If you can conscientise your intent, feel its energy, you may discover the real power of an intent that is generated in full awareness[1]. It is the signature, the *innate spirit* to be placed at the core of what you engage in. You may feel it grow as a tension that stays put within yourself. If so, refine it, focus it and feel this energy you are about to release in the act.

This intent awareness is the very image of what created the world. The very expression of *Dhat Allah*. This may give you an idea of how powerful this is.

In-tension.

Intent is the whole content of the act, pre-existent and perfect within our *presence* field.

Just like the forename of a child to be born.

We have no idea of how powerful, how light, how precise this impulse actually is. Intent defines the content of the world we live in, what is carried out by the circumstances we attract or the people we meet, and there is no more revealing experience

---

[1] You had better not express it by "I want, I wish…" rather by "the intent at the core of this act is…"

than to discover the link between an intent you have stated and the events that follow.

Every of us has this fine perception, which we use to a greater or lesser extent, to feel the intent behind a word or an act. For example, the intent you put in a dish while cooking will be felt by your guests, beyond the taste quality of its ingredients. It is the content of what you give them. If you experiment with this, you may be surprised at what they say.

It is therefore easy to comprehend that intent, much more than thought, is powerfully active at an immaterial level.

Thus, we carry on with our apprenticeship.

The power of form (*Sifat*)

Here manifests the nature of what is created, of the enterprise, of the vessel. Through the form, the destination manifests itself. **Form (nature) perfectly translates and manifests an intent that it adapts to circumstances, to contexts.**

Nature identifies with form.
Formalised intent becomes goal, *formal* destination.

The alignment between awareness, intent and circumstances translates into the perfect equilibrium of form. The formal perfection of a flower, of a shark or an oak tree shows how they are precisely fitted to their natures as well as contexts. And this equilibrium is dynamic: adaptation to everchanging contexts is continuous and endless.

The form/vessel bridges intent/content and circumstances. It is necessarily well adjusted and precise.
Form is what enables us, humans, to get organised between ourselves, the formal goal and the processes we set to ourselves.

As an example, if your intent is to transport goods to come to help to populations in need, the vehicle you build will be different whether it is bound to cross deserts, oceans or steep mountains. Form *comprehends* and integrates the context.

It is critical to take the time of form, to deepen your knowledge of the contexts, to meticulously define what is in and what is out, the limits of what you design. Then what you undertake can only be beautiful, powerful, the perfect manifestation of the intent it carries.

Time is inherent to the power of form. You must know and take the time of things, to weigh the act about to be carried out. Each nature, each accomplishment has its proper time and hastening things is one of the best ways to miss the point.
Usually at this stage, one may feel the glee, the joy in anticipation of what is being conceived and to come.

This power is so gratifying, so powerful that some of us merely satisfy themselves with it and stop there. The thing is conceived, it exists at the level of spirit, but it does not get born and remains in limbo.
What is needed, what makes it possible to bring an act to completion, what provides it with materiality in this world is the fifth power.

The power of resolution (*Asma*)

This power expresses, all at once, the *resolve,* the ability to *focus*[1] and the ability to find *solutions* to the difficulties we will undoubtedly encounter. That's how important it is.

This power enables us to interact with the subordinate forces: animals, vegetables and material. It is the one we are the most familiar with. The one by which we manifest ourselves on a physical plane.

The tiger tamer or the horse rider knows it well: one must show resolve in order to master an animal. The animal must feel it, and this is what generates respect. It goes the same with the ploughman, the logger or the craftsman: resolution is needed to work the earth, to cut wood or stones, to assemble cement and cinder blocks, to form metal, to put together a machine or to run a business. Any project calls for resolve

---

[1] One speaks of an « image resolution ».

and those who succeed at the material level all have demonstrated their resolution.

But resolution substantially differs from willpower. It is not of the same nature, it is calmer, made of confidence and not fear (even if surprises and difficulties are bound to happen), of love and respect for what is being used and completed, it is neither antagonism nor domination. Resolution works *with*, not *upon*.

An act is not a fight (against matter, elements, circumstances, others). It is an engagement, the projection of being, the apex of *presence,* of the intent and nature that are manifesting themselves, energised by resolution.

Your resolution is the mark of your coherence: if what you live is what you decided for (how could it be otherwise?), you must bring it to completion, what would be the point otherwise? If not, you build your life on a lie to yourself.

In that case, would not it be time for a change?

You may take all the time you need for reflexion as long as it may be, but come the moment to engage into action, you ought not to misuse your resolution power, it is an obligatory passage for all that gets born. Your resolution must be of the same quality as your intent.

Think of the mother's resolution when she gives birth. Or the sportsman's when he sets off, the musician's when she decides to break the silence. The sailor's in the storm or the climber's on his wall.

The moment of resolution is of real power and immense beauty. This is the moment when the times of preparation and the time of experience meet. **The moment when the living happens.**

This is the moment when the human being pierces through, makes the difference between what could be and what is. This is what gives the experience of this world its density.

Resolution is the seal of all the above, the tangible signature of love, awareness, intent and form.

I Am-ness

Thus, the act is born

"Between the act and matter, strikes the spark."

"Your work is your prayer." [xlv]

Every selfless act that is performed in awareness radiates far beyond the ego. Of such an act, one is no author, merely an interpreter.
An act that is real is performed **with no other purpose than to carefully do what life expects you to do**. Nothing more, nothing less. With no motivation of any sort.

Such an act does not belong to you (let alone its result!), exactly in the same way as music does not belong to the musician that plays it. An act is a potential within the *One-Presence*, that is discovered and actualised. **A gift**, whatever it is.

There joy is.

Every one of us acts, plays his or her score as we feel fit. Some put *their heart into it*, add a personal touch, the will or desire for something (perfection, result, satisfaction, experiment, pleasure or money...). Others take the measure of their intention and do for the sake of doing, for the act itself, they let themselves be guided by what it contains, even though it eludes them most of the time. They surrender to the instant guidance.

The experience of each one corresponds to what they get from it, but all do not have the same reality.

At the essential level, in Reality, there is no subject nor object, **object and subject are but one**. There is only verb.
Similarly, in an act that is purely performed in *presence*, cause and effect vanish. One acts neither "because" nor "for", one performs **an act for itself**, independently of an "*I*" or whomever.

It is critical to comprehend that the unescapable "cause-effect" relationship as we experience it, only exists in this world, not because of some divine decree but merely because of the one nature of Creation. In Reality all is one, the intent instantaneously merges with the result, but it has to pass through the act in order to be. It goes the same in our world, with the difference that space and time come into play **so that we have the time to understand the relationship between cause and effect.**

Subject, object, cause, effect proceed from the illusion of distance, of time and of separation. In the eternal instant of Reality, there is only the verb. Only the act.

This is precisely what Creation is: an accretion of acts, an accumulation of verbs. **Only the verb matters.** Reality is all verb, only the verb creates, the rest is but a story.
The verb only is experience, all else is a pretext to experience: subject, complement, circumstances...I, you, we, they,...all of these are illusion.

What you do to others, you do to yourself because separateness is illusion[1]. **To give and to receive is strictly the same act** and the only reason for separateness is to make the act possible in this world. This is the world sublime illusion: to perceive ourselves as separated, so that the experience of Creation *realises itself* [2].

---

[1] Which means that one always experiences the effects of one's acts, either in this life or in others.

[2] In both meanings of the word.

In the phrase *"I eat a salad"* neither *I* nor *a salad* exists in Reality. These are the very same Reality perceived through different *presence* prisms, distinct natures. Only *eat* manifests an intention, a variation in awareness, an act, **a change in energy and in *presence* all at once**: here from the vegetable *presence* plane (*Nabati*) to the physical human plane (*Jasmani*).

There is a wonderful phrase in a book that is just as much: "The beggar does you a favour when you give him one dollar. If he thanks you, it is for having given him the opportunity to do you a favour."[xlvi]

The Origin is sole *I Am-ness*. It only is endowed with the *I* identity. All the rest borrows it, plays it in a gigantic and diverse game.
Hence, be aware of who says *"I"* when you speak. It is always a borrowing, an usurpation most of the time. *"We"* is somewhat better. If you give it a closer look, at the end of the day there are neither reason nor opportunity to really say *I* without being mistaken.

Now you may comprehend that **an act is completely missed if performed for oneself**. The *"I"* is usurped and the share of the other misses. Just like an actor who rehearses in front of a mirror. It is fine, he may even play well but he misses the point really. To act for oneself, what a mistake! It is a misappropriation of who you are, of what you use, a diversion of both what is created as well as of That which creates.

Here something must be said: It is a sickly aberration to say, as one sometimes hears, that the Source begets Creation to contemplate Itself. This is sheer narcissism. The primeval Love-Intent is so negated in this, and Creation so utterly misconstrued, that this expresses a nothingness from which even It is absent.

The Source begets because It cannot do otherwise, it is Gift in all possible forms, this is precisely why Creation is endless. How could it be so beautiful otherwise?

This shows how important it is to complete an act in full awareness, as a gift whenever possible.

To act is to perform in *presence*, with intent (for the act), to engage into both form and resolution. Most of all, it is to be free, empty of self-interest, to be *in love*. In love with life as it enfolds within the act. There an act proceeds from *Presence*, leaves a trace for all eternity.

This is far easier to feel this when there is no money involved. If any money is at stake, if you are paid for an act, try and disconnect what you do from the revenue it generates, realise these are of two very distinct natures indeed: the act, the verb proceeds from eternity, a wage is obviously of this world.

Conversely, try not to pay someone for something you can do yourself. This would be a missed opportunity for both of you. If you have to, give money to the person for her needs, with no connection whatsoever with the act, and entrust her with the deed so that she can, in her turn, experience the subject/object-cause/effect conversation unmislead.

For this to happen, you had better choose people who are able to make this distinction, able to interpret the act on your behalf with as little self-interest and as much pleasure in the doing as possible. Then, the moment will benefit to everybody.

Whether you are raking leaves, cleaning your house, driving children to school, bringing comfort to a sick, or driving a bus, train or plane, you may feel the joy of being in act as if in love, you may experience this conversation with the forces, the *presence* planes that participate in it.

Gratitude rises, a flow that comes from the things you manipulate and goes to the Source. It passes through you; you are its channel, but it is not intended for you.
To selflessly act is your most beautiful way of doing. To selflessly act is to be.

Thus, the work is born.

The work originates in a selfless use of our five powers, with no ego involved whatsoever.
The work is an act that is complete, performed by a human fully guided, infused, inspired by the primeval *Intent to Be* which connects him/her to the source of all beings.

There is no point in coming to death without having been artisan of a work at least once. To perform a work is the purpose of a life. Master masons got this well, who had their apprentices walk and tour among fellow craftsmen until they became capable of a "master work". The Great Work, *Opus Magnum*, is not merely the proof that one masters matter, processes or gestures, it demonstrates a profound comprehension of how forces and realms organise themselves in the universe, the ability to let oneself be enacted, guided from the inner with no ego interference whatsoever. The ability to express the beauty of That which is, as faithful interpreters.

There is no such thing as a big or small work. Any act that is performed in a non-egotistic awareness state is work. This suffices to be human, and this is huge.

For example, to help someone cross a street[1].

The act that is complete expresses the perfection of what is, and this is precisely what makes it great: the work is perfect when it expresses the perfection of the Origin's Nature of Being.
It is so beautiful, so powerful that we give it a try all our life long.

Now you are at the core of your apprenticeship, what you try and reiterate every day.

Never do anything as a matter of routine. Never. Routine is the sister of materiality, of mechanisation. What you do today routinely will be done tomorrow by a machine. An act that repeats itself is a renewed opportunity to let the

---

[1] Provided that one does not do it to feel good, nice or generous. Provided that no feeling interferes with the act.

genuine work come into being. Each time, through each gesture, each thought.

Allow the work to get born through you, at the core of your thoughts, your acts, your hands, your words or body. All your senses contribute to the work provided that you do not take ownership of anything that is going on, as long as you let the *Intent to Be* which dwells at the deepest of yourself, behind the ego, act.

An act is only real in *presence*. The result, in Reality, of "building a house" is not the house. It belongs to this world. The house is **the illusion that is essential to the form and to the act**. What is real is "building". The whole process of awareness, intention, reflection, form, use and resolution. This orderly and well understood exchange between mineral, vegetal, (animal at times) and human natures.

What matters is what you are, what inhabits and enlivens you while you build. The result in Reality will be totally different depending on whether you are driven by a profit motive or greed, by the obligation to do (because of a salary or a creed), by an obsession with the time or money that is lost or saved, or moved by nothing, only fully present to the act itself. In the first cases, you operate in a materialistic, temporal and constrained *presence plane* while in the latter, you live a *presence* field that is free, detached, open and eternal.

Now you may distinguish an action from an act. An action is temporal, focused upon result, a sort of outer purpose, a form to be reached. An act is atemporal, it proceeds from *presence* and bears its result that is already there, if things are properly done.

Act with no impatience, without any specific mindset or expectation, with no other purpose than what you are doing.

Through an *act in presence*, you find yourself at the core of the world equilibrium, an equilibrium that is punctual and perfect, which you ought to ceaselessly look for, between the intent, the act and the circumstances. It is so perfect that it goes by itself, it flows naturally, everything falls into place in a timely manner.

Once you experience these synchronicities, these truly wonderful coincidences, you sense in yourself a powerful feeling of reality as much of unreality, the sense of another reality. As if an energy that is specific to the instant was *at work*. A moment that tells the perfection of form and "the alignment of the stars": all that which concurs to the act is thoroughly aligned: love, awareness, intention, form and resolution.

There you may be given the comprehension of how much you exhaust your strengths when you trudge against the course of the living.

Everything that is realised with this very feel of an act, nourishes the world as well as yourself. Talent is nothing else than this ability to perform an act *naturally*, with ease, joy and wonder.

Our actions whether "good" or "bad" tell our story, the one we want to share. They tell our ego, are only filled with that.

An act is of another nature, another *presence*. Our acts free ourselves from the ego, there is no "I", "you", "they", there is no possible good or evil. There is only what is currently done, whatever it is. **An act is a state of being, a state to the world.** All the rest is pointless. In that state, love uncovers, is given and received at its highest.

Just as unconditional love, the unconditional act tells you about where you come from. It is through the act that you best communicate with the Source.

Now you begin to understand what a world in worship could be. A world that is active, human, respectful of others and of life, a world where it is easy to feel well. A world of abundance through the work of humans.

To worship is to use the power of the act. It is not bowing down, turning toward this or that direction, toward this or that icon, going to this or that "consecrated" place, with hands clasped together, kneeling or with a bent back. Or worse, inflicting deprivation or pain to oneself. Worship is neither a feeling nor an attitude.

To work in awareness is to perform an act in Reality. To work is to worship[1].

To perform an act is to engage in this immense conversation with the Creator.

We all have a distorted perception of the notion of work, largely tainted by materialistic considerations or the occasional religious principles. Something like a social or even economical obligation, tasks to be performed "to

---

[1] To work translates in latin in *laborare: labor* work – *orare* pray.

earn a living"[1], that is to say money, to feed, shelter, dress, heal, educate or entertain ourselves. All rights that are intrinsically ours, which would be obvious in a genuinely humane world [2].

There is a profound beauty in the work-act, and it is time for human beings to free themselves from the perception of work as being the effect of an obligation or a cause for subjection. This materialistic perception is made of constraints, automatisms, trials of pain and endurance, coming along with its corollary of authority and subordination. It places us at the level of an obscure and materialistic awareness, opposite to whom we really are.

---

[1] This expression is so absurd that it can generate anger. The right to be alive is given to us *naturally*, it cannot be taken away to be reconquered by some labour at the service of someone or something exterior to ourselves.

[2] In a humane world, the right to live fully, decently is owned by anyone. Not depending on work, on the ability to perform an act which is an expression of self and a rightful conversation with Creation. It comes along with the notion of responsibility, however.

Work can only be the contribution, the share we take in experiencing the living. To be alive is to be in labour.

What we call abundance.

Each creation degree *works*, which means it carries out its functions in collaboration with the other planes. Work is the natural, spontaneous and noble expression of the sense of being. To work is merely to serve, to acknowledge, exercise and experience one's *presence* degree. The stone "works" when it participates in the balance of forces (for example in cathedrals), wood "works" when the carpentry finds its place and fulfils its role, the bee "works" when it forages, the human "works" when he/she creates, the woman is "in labour" when she gives birth.
Within the human body, myriads of cells, neurons and synapses, molecules and atoms "work", exercising their functions in full cooperation.

The idea of an "eternal rest" is a human invention. It comes from **the confusion between stillness-equilibrium and inertia**. The non-manifested planes of *presence* know no movement as they exist beyond space and time. They are in constant **equilibrium** but are neither inert nor inactive. They too live "in labour", they perform selfless acts (and justifiably so!) which carries both *Intent to Be* and *Sense of Being*. Acts that carry evolution across Creation.

I do not speak from myself; but the Father who abides in me, he does the works.[xlvii]

We now comprehend that these powers, as powerful they may be, are not ours. We are entrusted with them, we are custodians, usufructuaries.
We must know them to use them wisely and serve their bare owner to the best of our abilities. We borrow them as an actor grabs a prop before going on stage.

To act on behalf of. In the name of.

This suffices.

This is the only way to keep the ego at distance, to set free from our separations and our confinements: to accept the void, to perform our acts by letting ourselves be guided.
This is the only way to live in Reality, **knowing it is for the best of ourselves**, of our undertakings and their consequences.

There we are at the heart of *Wei Wu Wei,* act and not act.

"It is possible to be empty of oneself, free of egotistic desires, enmities and angers, envy, lust and vengeance, so that only God is in control of your heart and mind. Thence you enter this state of being directed by God. This is a state of glory, love, generosity and care for the others as much as you would for yourself, a state of non-judgment as you accept the others exactly as they are, children of God, equal in the Father's attention. It is a state of unbounded and unspeakable bliss, rejoicing for the beauty of the world." [xlviii]

I Am-ness

Our vehicles

Our thought form: The ego

What we come across, as soon as we look into ourselves, is our thought form, our ego.

It is the form, the attire, the shape in which we mould our *presence*, how we continuously translate *intent to be* and *sense of being*.

It is our deceitful shelter.
The (very) capable illusionist.

The ego is a construction that does not proceed from Reality. It is a **continuous interpretation of it,** in order to provide us with a reality on our own scale or sometimes excessiveness. Because the infinite is unbearable, unviable to us, the ego is a kind of space-time suit that we use to experience Reality. This is what we identify with.

The ego is what *translates,* according to <u>our own nature</u>, the nature of development, nourishment and protection of the Source. It feeds on it, just like a canal would store for itself most of the flow that goes through it.

Such a baffling online loss.

The ego is where our protections, projections and insatiable lusts originate from. It is this story of ourselves that we have erected and cling to, which we continuously enrich because we think it serves our own development and survival.

The ego is our way of making reality our own. But the more it reinforces itself, the more it covers reality up, that which it derives its own raison d'être from. Exactly as inhabitants of a city surrounded by walls which they continuously thicken for fear of *else*, we lock ourselves in, and come to experience a self-inflicted segregation, totally oblivious of the vast and magnificent world beyond.

The original *I Am-ness* is what activates the ego with a fabulous energy. The primeval *Intent to be* we bathe in, pushes the ego to act and react, to undertake and engage into improbable adventures which all are creation experiences. It is because of it that the ego works very hard to continuously, and as much as possible, reinforce our sense of being.

The ego is the ultimate survival kit that perfectly fits our *presence* state.

Its raison d'être is to ensure our survival and augment our sense of being. It filters all that comes from Being according to our own *presence* degree, **so that we feel alive according to our own standards**, to fabricate a world that is both accessible and proportionate to what we believe we are, where to blossom and thrive while defending us from what it considers a threat. It is **constant evaluation and judgment**, sifting what comes to us to keep what is "good" for us and discard what is "bad".

It is the inevitable artisan of our separateness. All the misery of the world comes from our incapacity to differentiate individuation from separation, due to our lack of proper tools to grasp it.
Yet it is possible to be individuated and NOT separated. This is the very nature of the *One-Awareness*. The very nature of *us*. To be at the same time all and a part of all.

The ego only perceives, only conceives and considers the part of all, "our" part. It is therefore easy to comprehend how it soon becomes a continuous self-reinforcement of our illusion about ourselves.

As an interpreter of Reality, it projects it according to our awareness field, it keeps reacting to it as a constant projection-reaction force. The impact of its projections as well as the *feed-back of* our senses, the circumstances, as well as what it understands of them, generate impressions, emotions and thoughts which, in their turn, imprint our awareness field and add to the ego's "interpretation stockpile", in **an endless positive feed-back loop**.

To perceive, act and interact through the ego reinforces it and turns it into a very effective locking device. We get trapped within our space-time suits.

As a self-confirmation of what we believe we are, the ego tirelessly generates an awareness field that is partitioned, separated from Reality, disconnected from the Source, which becomes autonomous. This restricted awareness field sediments and imprints our deep being and **we end up becoming what we believe we are**.

And the cycle goes on and on and on[1].

A cause-effect cycle sets into place: our *presence* field, confined by the ego as by a straight-jacket, constantly determines the intentions we can state. These, as well as the acts which follow, generate a reality which, as it is interpreted by the ego, imprints in its turn our awareness field and, in doing so, ascertains its own validity. Day after day, intention after intention, action after action, we fashion the awareness state where we "choose" to vibrate.

We "create" the reality of the world we live in.

Incarnation after incarnation.

Egos, in their turn, attract and repel each other (Remember, their purpose is evaluation and judgment). From these attractions, our creeds, dogmas, truths, certainties about us and the world get born. From these repulsions come our antagonisms of all kinds, our aversions, our conflicts and wars.
From these accumulated stories, our cultures, societies and civilisations get born.

---

[1] The Hindus'Maya.

All these stories that apparently tell us and confirm who we are.

The whole human drama.

Is it not astounding that we call this *history?* Does it not say it all? All that we have fabricated and that we believe is solid, true, certain, long lasting, all that we deem our own determination, at the end of the day is but a story we tell ourselves.

There you may comprehend that your awareness states, your intentions and actions, your preoccupations and agitations only define a route, an itinerary, a specific experience within an infinity of possible *presence* fields. They define the re-creation ground where each of us plays. Or the floor in the shopping mall.

"If your present consciousness is permeated with love of possessions and an inability to share with others, devising ways and means to become rich at the expense of others, stealing, failing to perform your work conscientiously or give good value for money, snapping, snarling, indulging in criticism, sarcasm, judgementalism, rejection, denigration, enmity, intolerance, hatred, jealousy, aggression, violent impulses, thieving, falsehoods, double and

devious dealings, slander – you are ego-driven. Your ego is in control, and you will find it difficult to move through the miasma of ego-consciousness to be able to see Reality."[xlix]

Here you may as well understand how vain it is to want to change the ego. On the contrary, the more you get interested in it or, worse, assail it, the stronger it becomes. The ego is a very efficient and very sophisticated self-development and self-defence program, at the service of your nature, of your *presence.*

In the image of an archer with his bow, arrow and target, the ego is the bow, where our desires and repulsions spring from. Do not blame the bow if you do not like the result on the target, it is just a tool. You would rather focus on the archer, your own nature to which the bow responds. Contemplate what it is made of, see all these prints and traces of various awareness planes which it is occupied with.

Be aware of your *presence.*
This, you will always come back to.

The life of a human being can only be a path in awareness, as it is in our very own nature to be called upon to evolve in it.

The ceaseless work of the ego is at the same time clumsy, respectable and tragic:
Clumsy because it keeps trying with stubborn naiveness, most of the time misusing the tools we have been given.
Respectable as any organ that supports our life, and more to the point, it is our very own space-time suit which we must care for.
Tragic as, while it believes it addresses our deepest needs, it is yet doomed to fail. No realisation whatsoever in this world will ever satisfy the unmeasurable urge for being that stems from the Origin, that is consubstantial with Creation.
Because the *Intent to be* is infinite by nature. To contemplate it is a vertiginous mise en abyme. It traverses us as an irrepressible, untouchable, unmeasurable impulse.

In order to really *be*, you must set your *intent to be* free from any dye or taint. To want not, to imprint not, to become fully transparent. To let the *Intent to Be* express through what you are. To live completely in the detachment of selfless awareness.

Dig a hole as deep as you can within the ego, and let water surge and rise. Then you will have made a well.

The "*I*" rises and manifests, a genuine individuated sense of being, your deepest being, your true reality.

Hence you may comprehend that the true "*I*" is not yours, it traverses but does not come from your ego, which is a mere witness to it. It is the complete expression of the *Sense of Being* within and through you[1].

Your true *I* at the deepest of yourself is non-ego, your being with no story, nor veil, nor want. Your being of all eternity.

This *being* is a fold, a wave, an infinitesimal variation within the *One-Awareness*, what religions call "the soul", our immortality. It borrows "its" *presence* to *I-am ness*. It is but a wrinkle at the surface of *Being*, like a ripple created by the wind. Each wave seems unique, bestowed with a life of its own whereas it is just an agitation of the sea by an energy input. A moment in the swell.

In our world, this *awareness fold* takes form. It needs a tangible form in order to be. This will be

---

[1] « *Only God is I* » (Wei Wu Wei – op.cit.) – see *YHWH* as well (*I Am Who I Am*)

our ego (psychic form) and our body (physical form).

It is easy to understand that these variations are at the same time all and parts of all. The facets and the jewel at the same time. The individuated part cannot be separated from the indivisible whole.

This is the ultimate miracle of Creation, all at once **fully realised and perpetually in progress**.
It is *realised* when seen from the Source perspective. The All is, of all times and all eternities. It cannot be otherwise.
It is *in progress* when seen from the perspective of an individuated awareness state, which realises it through intention, form and act. It cannot be otherwise.

This is the miracle of experience.
The unconceivable reality we daily live: the *present* of the living.

To be in *I Am-ness* that is not self.
Am-awareness.
Only a verb, here again.
Nothing more, nothing less.

Realisation is precisely the *realisation* that there is no *I*.

Realisation implies the annihilation of any form given to the sense of being. When realised, one can only be, one cannot even be *I am* aware. Only the Source radiates *I am*, all the rest is.

To be without getting born.

To serve.

In absolute stillness, the ego does not exist.[i]

The only possibility to be, to act and to think in equilibrium and at peace is to surrender. It is to comprehend that the *Intent to Be* and *Sense of Being* that inhabit us, come from the Source, are completely beyond us. We merely are their interprets as we would of a gigantic sound that echoes from and to nowhere.

By experiencing surrender, you may let yourself be touched by the Source, beyond the ego, and let it drive your intentions, your impulses, your acts. Therein you are fulfilled.

There is no unfulfilled desire. There are only unfulfilled humans.[ii]

Go to the source of wonder.

And by-pass all the ego illusory, complicated and self-justifying machinery.

Detachment is an awareness state that is open, free and complete. It is neither astonishment (which implies separateness) nor want (which implies willpower). It bears within itself gratitude and wonder, the feel of perfection of what Is, the feel of being in Reality.

The All perceives all, the part only perceives the part, but it is always about the Source. There is nothing else. The part is restless, it can but move around in its own *presence* field, or possibly journey between them by letting go.

Every part of creation serves a purpose, all is rightly at its place. There is no truth. Everything is true.

Lying

The laws of the universe are exact, precise, immutable.
Lying is the ego that manifests itself, an ego that always alters reality to its own profit. To lie is to wilfully get out of the real, to believe one can defy

or escape the law of responsibility, to create one's own little world whether enjoyable or defensive. This is delusion, folly, separateness from oneself.

There is no such thing as a "good" reason for lying. None. To lie is to let oneself get lost in the illusion of self as in a labyrinth. Not to lie is neither a social, moral nor religious obligation. This is not a commandment as if prohibited "from Above" either.

It is the reality of what we are that makes it impossible to lie.

A lie is only a manoeuvre from an ego that wishes to be in command, that believes it can fabricate a world that protects oneself. It only locks us within the illusion of a separated world. That, sooner or later, we will want to get away from.

If you *really* want to understand something in what happens to you, in what you live and feel, do not fabricate these petty trivial individual truths which merely are misguidance and mediocre separations. Start with accepting what life signals to you under the form of circumstances, encounters and events, take responsibility for what you are and live. Hence you will start deciphering the signal of Reality from your own personal noise.

Our judgements

Judging is the ego basic tool, which constantly evaluates, weighs, compares, arbitrates, absolves and condemns. Most of the time in our own favour.[1]

Judging is consubstantial with our sense of being when interpreted by the ego. Judging is just like breathing, it is so natural that we forget about it. It sets the boundary between self and else, between what one is and what one is not.

Judgment is the cloth our space-time suit is made of.

"What's this guy?... Who does she think she is?... Away you go!... Why him...Poor me!... Get lost!... What does she have more than me?... This is not normal!... Always the same ones!... "They" are nuts!... It's all the big non-sense...What a b...!" Our daily lives are littered with these little cookie-cutter separations which we mutter to ourselves or

---

[1] Or in our disfavour in the case of a reversed ego, where the sense of being translates into being "less".

shout out loud, notwithstanding our gossiping when we swarm around them.

To judge is to position yourself versus the other, to determine whether she/he contributes to or hinders your sense of being. This continuous evaluation is the most obvious mark of the vegetable awareness field that is at work within us and holds us within a sub-human *presence* state.

To judge is the ego's exercise of choice in order to stay fit. Just like going to the gym.

Our convictions

The ego is the undisputed champion of being right. Being right is our ego-translated *sense of being*.
To be right upon others is the most trivial and immediate expression of our animal nature. And when we add to this the obtuse inflexibility of matter, then we stand at the core of separateness and confinement.

When we think we are right, when we see the error in the other, when we want to persuade others of our rightness, when we believe we are "more" (competent, shrewd, powerful, generous, understanding... whatever comes to mind), when, with our thoughts, projections or acts, we belittle the other or create pain or confusion...all these intentions contribute to seeing ourselves separate and proceed from the chief illusionist.

To *be in the right* is to choose not to be *in presence*, to separate from what Is.

The only possibility is to *be with*, with no preference or desire, and let life take its course.

When you debate, exchange or build with others, just lay your opinions, intentions or ideas down amidst the others', observe them live and see what they become, in this instant or later. In your turn, seize the others' opinions, intentions or ideas, observe them in the same way, listen to what they tell you without being hooked by the drive to evaluate, want or persuade. Get along, be the movement and seize the opportunity to be useful. Wherever it comes from. What is real always comes back to the surface, in due time, and what is not disappears and it does not matter.

Our desires

Do not negate or disparage your desires, your longing or need for pleasure or felicity:

"They are destitute relatives, but they come from good stock."[lii]

They are images of Reality, distorted most of the time, confusing at some, but images all the same of what we are given to experience, once the mask is dropped. The energy that drives desire is what the universe is born from, an awesome might within us.
The whole point is to decipher which source it originates from, what intention it contains.

When it originates from Reality, desire is impulse, magnificent and mighty.
The energy of the stream that continuously flows from the Source is magnificent, do not blame it for being laden with the litters and scraps that are rejected by those who camp on its banks.

Question your desires and love your impulses.

Your desires are the most reliable messengers of what you are, of your nature and *presence.* Do start a conversation with them, ask them to tell you about who you are, acknowledge what they do to others as if it were to yourself. Let this awareness grow within you, this is just enough to change, if time for a change has come.

At the end of the day, you will realise you just have to be, there is nothing to want, nothing to transform. Desire just becomes what it is: the expression of a life force whatever it is. You experience being and all happens unknowingly.

In the story of the archer and arrow, desire is the arrow. Once again, if you have a problem with the target, change the archer.

An impulse is a desire that has neither expectation, object nor subject. One merely lets oneself be traversed by it. Impulse is part of being, it leads into acting for the sake of the act while, on the other hand, desire is a want that takes us out of ourselves.

A selfless impulse is pure expression of the *Intent to Be* that is not filtered by the ego. Unlike desire that can be imperious, unruly, violent even according to the nature it originates from, impulse is discrete, elusive, easy not to be acted upon.

Yes, the Universe is only abundance and satisfaction of needs, yes, it is an awesome garden where we may actualise our dreams, but we first have to get in tune, to raise our *presence* to where all is in its place, to where we can just be filled by the marvellous order at work within Creation. **There all our dreams are merely what is.**

When your demands come from a feeling of lack, of frustration, anger, revenge or confinement, they serve no one, particularly not you. In a consciousness of lack or greed, desire is always a manifestation of separateness: separateness between what you are and what you wish for, separateness between you and the object, separateness between you and others.

A desire that comes from lack, locks you in lack, whether it is satisfied or not. An impulse that comes from joy, keeps you in joy, whether it is satisfied or not.

If your asking is in gratefulness even before it is satisfied, an impulse arising from gratitude, then you connect with Creation in its real nature, and all comes to you. It cannot be otherwise. It is no longer an asking but a receiving rather, merged with a gift, a state of joy and acceptance. There, the universe's profusion manifests, abundance appears, and "miracles" set into place.

Lack is a state of mind generated in man's consciousness. If you look for abundance, start with creating it around you. Reverse the desire and transform it into an impulse. Give, give anything, time, money, talent, food, attention, prayer. Transform yourself into a source of abundance, do not seek that it serves you, do not get in the way, let all things and bounty pass through you.

As soon as we become interpreters of abundance, it manifests around us. We live abundance and, by the very effect of its nature, we benefit from it in our turn.

Just as when you eventually decide to speak the language of a country you would have chosen to live in. Until you speak the language, it is difficult to orientate, find a job or a place where to live, to get food or care, to entertain and get your various needs met. You experience lack under many different forms. As soon as you speak the language, everything becomes natural, easy, people and circumstances naturally come to you, smile at you, you belong.

To ask is natural when it expresses trust in the living, in the Divine. As in a conversation. As when asking "can you pass me the salt, please?" This request does not stem from lack, it is just **a need that you do not doubt for a moment that it will be met**. And of course, it is. If, on the other hand, your request comes from a sense of lack or separateness, as if the Divine had forgotten or neglected you (*please, please, please!*) it will be satisfied just like the other (the Source does not judge) but the response will come under a form you will not recognise because your *presence* state will not make it possible. For instance, as an opportunity you will not even notice. Or a crisis.

Our physical form: the body

Until now, we have extensively talked about awareness. Now it is time we speak of energy. Which is just the same considered from the perspective of this world.

Energy is the form which *presence* takes in our world. It is everywhere, around and within us, at the core of everything, under very diverse and subtle forms whether perceptible or not. In the void even.

Very few people are aware of their body as a form of **energy-awareness**. Not the energetic form we indulge in by sweating, muscles exertion and endocrine agitation, rather the shape we all take in this world, our nature (*Sifat*). Remember, nature and form are inseparable: they are the very same expression of the *Sense of Being* that bears/is Creation.

Our body is the projection of our sense of being under the form of energy. It expresses in this world, with its own language, the perfection that we are[1]. Whichever form it may be.

Energy is awareness made tangible in the realm of substance. And the vehicle for this transformation is **information**, constantly exchanged within and without our body. Information is a quantum of awareness[2], an awareness bit, the very fundamental building block of Creation[3]. When we eat, breathe, digest, walk, sleep, talk, write, act, we exchange information between different awareness fields, we *assimilate* and transform the mineral, vegetal, animal, physical human planes within their energetic as well as *presence* levels. We participate in the gigantic game of energy-awareness. we generate movement between awareness degrees and *that* is very precisely Creation in the making.

When you consider your body (or any body or thing), you see, touch, smell, hear, taste, perceive *presence* in a form that is at the same time tangible (energy) and intangible (information). **Our body is**

---

[1] Perfection is not a value-judgment, only the statement that whatever form Creation may take, it is utterly ordered.

[2] One could say that ultimately quantum mechanics describes phenomena at the awareness level.

[3] Cf note 2 page 131

a dazzling aggregate of energy/information at work. Energy is awareness that is perceived in a tangible way, while information is awareness that is apprehended in an intangible manner. It is all about awareness. We are witnesses of how Creation works at our awareness/*presence* level.

This simply is astounding.

We are energy/information transformers. Our body/mind captures and transforms the energy/information that diffuses in the whole Creation, the innate energy of the ultimate *I Am-ness* as we can perceive it. This energy[1] is cold like the energy of the absolute void. It warms up when it manifests, when it enlivens and flows, when it becomes the *Qi* energy, the heat of which we can feel as soon as we activate and store it.

In our manifested world, awareness is energy, hence the sub-human planes we are given to use and *assimilate* are awareness fields and forces as much as energy sources.

Your human body itself is a perfect and continuous balance between awareness and energy, between

---

[1] The *Jing* energy, the vital essence in Taoism.

the energies of "Heaven" and those of "Earth". This is where an intense circulation takes place between "high" and "low", between "inside" and "outside", between how you feel (sense of being) and your physical energies. Everything circulates within you and through you, in an osmosis of awareness/energy planes you do not have the faintest idea. **Your body is a lump of energy/information, just as you are a lump of awareness.** And these two lumps constantly superpose, merge, interact, because they are the same reality seen from different perspectives.

To be alive in this world is to constantly exchange and transform energy into awareness and the other way round.

The body/mind is where **awareness transmutes into energy** in a circulatory and continuous manner, as told by the Taoist tradition: awareness projects energy just as energy is awareness on the move. All begins with *Wuji,* the absolute void where awareness inseminates energy, gives birth to energy-awareness, just like the spermatozoid inseminates the ovule. From then on, Taoism acknowledges three energy types: *Jing,* the cold vital essence, *Qi,* the circulatory hot energy, *Shen*, the active awareness. To live, breathe, move or eat is to set the Taoist alchemy in motion: to transform

Jing into *Qi* then into *Shen* and come back to *Wuji*, the end of the energy-awareness transmutation[1]. *Wuji* as a beginning and an end all at once.

All along extends the path to *active awareness*, like DNA curled within itself.

Mobilis in immobile.

A permanent information transmutation takes place, in a continuous balance between awareness and energy, between inner and outer, between the individual and cosmic energies. the awareness-energy dynamics of the manifested world.
At our human level, this manifests within the physical body. There, this equilibrium takes place. Our body is this magnificent vessel where awareness-energy activates and deploys. We are the place of a daily miracle, and we are unaware of it.

Our body is perfection of form, precisely matching our human nature, as it is conceived in *I Am-ness*. It is protection, nourishment, work, satisfaction of needs, equilibrium, order and rhythm.

---

[1] This is the basis of *Qi Qong,* a millenary Chinese spiritual/physical exercise (awareness/energy).

It is the most accessible medium by which to witness the perfection of Creation.

Our conversation with Creation begins in our body: we protect it, nourish it, make it work, meet its needs, keep it in balance, maintain its order and rhythm. Just as it protects, nourishes, keeps us in balance, maintains our rhythms and provides to our needs.

Everything is in place for anyone wishing to understand the orderly perfection of what is.

From the balance of energies within our body comes its ability to heal itself[1]: the healing of wounds, the regeneration of cells and tissues, the elimination of toxins are the daily demonstration of this self-healing capability.

Far from marvelling at it, we have gradually lost our respect for the human body, replaced (at best) by hedonism in western societies, a kind of compulsive and narcissistic adulation of our appearance and physical *form*. We play with it, manipulate it, decorate it, submit it to all kinds of practices, sometimes strange or painful, according to our cultures or traditions, but who does *really* see what it is?

---

[1] Suffices to watch how, when wounded, an animal puts himself at rest...and heal.

The human body is not this machine we can use at will, of which we can change parts upon demand or nearly. All this proceeds from a mechanistic, materialistic vision that is separated from the living. Our body is an image in seven dimensions (including the mind and emotions), which supports our *presence* field. This is not about beauty, aesthetics, performance or efficiency. Nor is it about flaws, weaknesses or handicaps. What may appear as a weakness or handicap is solely the projection of a standard, hence a materialistic thought. Weaknesses and handicaps are as powerful and perfect expressions of the Intent to Be as any others.

Your bodily envelop is precisely fitted to what you came to achieve in this world, to your purpose.

When you enter in this curious, joyful and attentive conversation with your body, you set off onto the discovery of this equilibrium, of what enlivens you, what you really are.

It first happens within, at the awareness level, before it manifests on the outside in your health, in your cravings and needs. If you observe an unbalance, a lack or an addiction, you may search within yourself, in the secret of your deep being, what it may originate from.

In order to really heal, you must understand as an awareness unbalance, the disturbance of energies you witness.

To heal is to identify a tension or a mismatch between your *presence* plane and what you manifest, between your intent to be and sense of being, between your nature and your acts, between what inhabits you and what you express.

Just as, for a given ailment, the Chinese medicine may diagnose an excess or lack of wood, fire, earth, metal or water energies, he/she who cares about what Is, may interrogate the inner balance of the mineral, vegetal, animal, human *presence* planes, explore how the ego distorts the purpose, where the disorder may come from.

We may witness this reality any time in our daily lives: when we exchange information, when we engage in a conversation, when we face circumstances, we may feel the energy surface, the very energy of information that is present in any *presence* degree, which, most of the time, is focalised *by* intent. **The mood in which our exchanges or conversations end tells us about the** *presence* **degree our mutual intents originate from**: it may be disease, rage, tears or laughter as well as well-being, peace, joy or bliss.

And here comes another "fact of life": the quality and quantity of information you feed yourself with has a direct and profound effect on how you feel, hence upon your health; quality tells you how the information (energy) you absorb fits or not with your own *awareness* degree, how it impacts the very fine equilibrium between the *presence* fields that composes your own sense of being (a mix of materialistic, vegetal, animal and human degrees...). Quantity tells you how too much information may make you sick, just as too much food makes you nauseous. By constantly watching television or any other screen, by devouring news *unaware*, you gradually alter your awareness field, and these changes may translate into disorders and illnesses.

Our moods which are expressions of ego, are hot-tempered when activated by the material, vegetal or animal energies; they are even-tempered when activated by human energies and freshen when activated by higher and subtler energies. The thoughts that agitate us generate heat, just as molecules do, because molecules are primarily just that: information/awareness aggregates. The lower the *presence* "frequencies" in us, the "hotter" the energy they generate. The wider the awareness degree, the more information it can embrace, the stabler it becomes, the more it enfolds complexity and the "fresher" (*cool*) it becomes.

And **this** tells us something about ourselves. Just as fever signals that the body is reacting to some alien disturbance, **our tempers signal awareness fields that are misplaced or misused within us**. Our moods mirror our ego, they are occasions of contemplating it. Yet another occasion of growing in awareness.

If you want to put your body at rest, start with putting your thoughts at rest. Then, you connect with the *presence* of the primeval Sense of Being (*Mother*) within you.

Now and here, you may understand how your body and ego influence each other, what they tell you about the great game of *active awareness*, the awesome game of life.

As well as the sheer *energy-awareness* that gives birth to all of this[1].

Because your body is the form taken by your *presence* degree in this world, it changes by itself if you evolve in *presence*. Thus, you may experience the betterment of your vital functions, of your *vitality*. Inspirations will come which have perceptible impacts on your physical form.

However, our body which is born, which is our form in this world, will not get into the "here-after". It is our vessel in this perceptible reality, it proceeds from an image.

When we die, energy and *presence* disjoint, and each go back to its own world. Our *presence* lives on at the degree that we manifested at the end of our lifetime, while the energy lump of our body desynchronizes from *presence* and diffuses into the energy field of this world. As for the form this momentarily awareness-energy fusion took to

---

[1] The deeper we dive into matter, the further we look into the cosmos, the more energy we uncover. Just consider the unspeakable energy that is needed to break apart (separate) subatomic particles or to expand a whole universe!

complete our purpose, it can but disappear. *Presence* is what remains.

What is born dies, what is not born cannot die.[liii]

I Am-ness

EXPERIENCING
LETTING GO

I Am-ness

Life is alive!

All the above has been about knowledge, with may be a few sensations at times. An active reality has been described which may occasionally have resonated with your own inner truth. Then you may have been engulfed in flashes of sudden awareness, surges of understanding.

A whole personal path has shown, to be followed.

Now it is time to move on to **experience**, to explore how we may feel and practise this reality in our daily lives. Because *ab initio* and *in fine*, any *presence,* whatever its degree, cannot but experience life. Life is the purpose of Creation, the experience of Creation in all its variety and eternity.

Remember: what we know has neither importance nor reality in this world. What is real is what we do with it.

Here comes the moment when to engage into the living.
Now is the time to make a choice.

After journeying through the above and with all what you know, you have to conscientiously choose your own experience mode, your very specific way of witnessing Reality in this world.

In full consciousness.

On the one hand, you may want to experience the infinite capacity of the universe to respond to any of your needs. You may wish to feel the pleasure and fertile joy of seeing it answer whatever expectations, requests and interrogations you may have, **in such ways that you growingly feel you are in control.**
Because the universe always answers when asked. All ways.

There are mighty invisible forces at work in the universe that can be put at service. These forces participate in the different *presence* states above mentioned and human beings have learnt how to connect with them and manipulate them (for instance, with occultism and shamanism).

This path of mastering things and circumstances is a path of power, sometimes called *the way of the sorcerers*. It is a path where one seeks results and works hard to achieve them, an inner transformation that is fully directed towards control and achievement. That is a path of willpower and influence upon things and beings, a path of mastering. A path wherein to experience **the satisfaction of feeling one's power and sensing it grow.**

It may well be that you have an interest in these things, you may wish to feel in control, that you grow your knowledge, you gain in influence, you master your life and your trajectory amongst events, circumstances, and people. And there is absolutely nothing wrong with that.

However, this will not be discussed here, this is not the purpose of this little book. There is no knowledge of this sort here.

In that case, it is likely that we come to the end of our journeying together, as what follows will not resonate with you nor what you are looking for, and books and opportunities that deal with this path come in the many, which will be more useful to you.

On the other hand, you may wish to experience total trust, to surrender to the living, to life with no other intention than to be at its service, with patience, sincerity, letting go and a real ability to surrender.

To be a channel.
To try, to always try to be just that.

To learn, listen and let yourself be guided by That which is beyond and precedes your ego. To put all your intellectual, relational, working capabilities, all what you are and are capable of at the service of That which is, precedes and contains all. Recognize you are an usufructuary and not owner of your life, a created being more than a creator. Experience yourself as an interpreter and not author of your life. Experience **the joy of serving.**

Act **with** what comes to you. Perform acts at the best of your talents (your five powers aligned) without appropriating the result, without expecting or rejoicing upon "successes", without fearing or being put off by "failures". In this path, you come to understand that your wrong doings, misfortunes and inadequacies are perceptions of the mind and always come from interferences of your ego. Always.

Learn
And be thankful.

Learn how to constantly be at a place and a state of mind where you are a miracle for others and leave it to life to make them for you.

Through selfless actions, he [the Master] attains fulfilment.[liv]

There, you engage into the path of letting go, sometimes called *the way of the prophets*. There, you may recognize yourself in what follows.

Of course, there are lots of in-betweens, moments when you want and instants when you let go. It happens all the time. But this only demonstrates you are still an apprentice: the intermediary way which would allow a bit of this and a bit of that leads to nowhere, it is an illusion, a dead end. At the end of the day, you must choose - or let life choose for yourself. Each path is a reality that requires you to fully engage into it, without regret nor hesitation. With complete determination for the former, in full confidence for the latter.

With joy either way.

This choice is yours. Try and feel what corresponds to your nature and purpose in life at this very moment. This is truly worth it.

And if you read on, you know that what is to come proceeds from not-wanting. From stepping into selflessness.

Daring.
Yes, but daring what, precisely?

Dare not to master, not to think you are in control, just that you are of service.
Dare to act, undertake with all your capacities, all these wonderful talents you carry and make you unique, while accepting you do not own the results. They just tell you how correctly you tuned your being.
Dare to be *in* love without expecting anything in return.
Dare the joy in the instant, without wishing to be reassured at the same time.
Dare gratitude, to thank with no reason, merely because you know that everything is in place, and you are irresistibly drawn to yours.

Dare not to do, to stay still and be guided by silence.

Dare to let go of the noise of your thoughts, of what constantly stirs you, your creeds, truths, preferences or wishes and *to uncover* silence. To unveil silence and *know* that there dwells That which makes us act in Reality.

Dare to be touched by this *Presence* that comes from nowhere in you and yet is there.
This is so tenuous, delicate, discreet, nothing clamorous, imperious nor evident[1]. This is an everyday exercise, the work of a life. An apprenticeship.

"The Teacher said, "My Father lives in secret".
He has said "Enter in your chamber, close the door,
And pray to your Father who is there in secret".
This means: in your innermost being,
That which is inside, in the secret of all, is fullness
Beyond it is nothing, it contains all.[iv]

Remember: to access *I Am-ness,* to let it infuse your existence, you have to bypass the ego whereas it reinforces as soon as you care about it.

---

[1] The Source does not speak. **It touches.** God does not need words nor intermediaries. Each time something or someone speaks in the name of God, or worse tells it/he/she is God (!!), we had better not listen and take distance, this is a decoy, this does not come from the Source.

There is a kind of impossible loop, a contradiction in terms that all those who tried, have come up against.

The only possible way is to let That do the work, the primeval *I Am-ness* wherefrom we get our own sense of being and that lives within all beings.

Start from your inner silence, wherefrom your most exquisite intentions and inspirations get born.

Here too, the paths that lead there are many, such as various forms of meditation for instance. As you are on your way, no doubt you will find yours, if you have not yet. Just stay as much as possible in an attentive peace (search and not search).

Let joy be your guide.
The joy of trust and letting go.

What is described in the following pages is a particular exercise of letting go, one among quite a few, an active one that is rather disconcerting by its simpleness. It results in a life experience that is usual and yet feels guided and somehow protected, a golden thread to walk along on the path of being human in the world.

There is no need for efforts, no rituals nor master. The path unfolds within, in perfect balance with the life propositions that daily come to you, these instants where you may become aware of your own *presence*. An apprenticeship in progress. The only possible master is the inner being which dwells at the innermost of yourself, which manifests through all that comes to you. Provided you can let it touch you and guide you.

A life experience, that is.

If you practice it long and assiduously enough, it will not turn you into a guru nor into some kind of master. Yet, it will take you to the edge of the *Rohani* being. The real, accomplished human being[1].
If this does not speak to you, if you do not feel the tenuous and vibrant drive to know more about it, other paths exist, which will come in due time and take you to the very same place.

In our apprenticeship of real human beingness, this exercise is a guide from the inner, in perfect and constant resonance with what comes from the outer. It opens to the *One-Awareness* in ourselves, at the core of our beings. It lets us be touched by

---

[1] Cf. page 150

the *Idhafi* vibration of life which alone can clarify our ego without us bothering about it.

With this exercise, we may experience a life at the deepest of ourselves, that is silent, imperceptible and constantly active. A Life within life. A life that is patently alive.

The loving intelligence of the Living.

Thus, very gradually and at your very own pace, you open to the content that you bear and that you are. You transform without having to want to.

The only real way to act is to let the act get born within yourself. The only real way to be is to let the being emerge from within. Do what circumstances call for but not be the cause for it. To the least possible.

To act *with* what comes (ideas, insights, events, people...any life proposition) but not search or will for it. Just to be at your place within the flow. And engage with your five powers.

Practicing surrender is everywhere and nowhere all at once.

It is *everywhere* as it is constantly necessary to cultivate letting go, to leave *our* preferences, judgments, evaluations, creeds and certainties behind. Our ceaseless conversations about ourselves, about life and the others.

It is nowhere because it cannot be voluntary, it cannot come from willpower or the ego, it has to come by itself.

All of the sudden, in doing so, it dawns onto you that life is alive, really alive and extraordinarily intelligent: it has a life of its own and you may just as well let it express itself and leave the controls to it.

At this point you have forded, reached the opposite riverbank and you did not even notice.

Then on, you trust life, you are continuously thankful with no reason, even before having a reason to be so [1]. Even when what happens to you is not so pleasant.

Then on, you let the living act in you.
And then on, you learn how never to get impatient, which is the most difficult for us, beings in need for proofs, reassurance and immediate results.

---

[1] If you perceived how instantaneous the Real is, you may understand why, in reality, the being is perpetually in gratitude: thankfulness and the reason to be so, are simultaneous.

Life is living intelligence. Make sure you discover this for yourself if you have not already. This is such an experience when it suddenly dawns upon you!

You could see it as a little girl at a friend's place, a toddler you barely know, who says nothing but keeps inviting you to play with her. She keeps coming to you with all sorts of propositions while you are chatting with her parents, she keeps presenting her toys to you, puppets, baubles and scribbles, one after the other. And most of the time, you welcome them distractedly, absent-minded because you think you have better to do or are engaged into something that is more of your concern, a conversation, a task, a project or preoccupations of your own. At worse you take that for a whim, something random; at best you acknowledge briefly and move on with what you were doing.

But if you pay attention and welcome the invite, if you share one game, then another and another, you discover a whole world. An intelligence of things, intuitions, ideas, encounters or circumstances that associate and connect to each other so nicely; a whole story takes shape and makes sense. Something to learn and that brings real deep joy.

All the joy you can see in her eyes for having shared her world, even for a moment.

Life is just that: a persistent and discreet invitation, so easy to dismiss, to discover a whole world, provided that you forget the one you are used to, even for just a while.

Life is this active *presence* we are immersed in, something immensely wise, which one ought to try and listen to and understand, a new language which is not foreign.

Yes, life is alive. Instead of seeing it inert, instead of believing in the accidental pile of non-sensical randomness from which only the human mind, willpower and determination make sense, you may, for a time, choose to take this for real, see what it brings forth, what you learn from it.

No life experience is useless, all are meaningful, most notably the unpleasant ones. Each is an opportunity to learn something about who we are and if we miss a few or many, they will show again on our path. Under another form.

Nothing is unsignificant. Insignificance is but a perspective from the ego, only preoccupied with itself.

We are dealing with an unmeasurable intelligence, capable of enfolding and expressing meaning within innumerable interactions between countless circumstances and billions of human beings, interactions where chance has no place, except for the ignorant we are.
All that happens to you has a meaning. All that happens is a life experience.

All.

In every moment, huge or minute, happy or sad, brutal or smooth, deliberate or endured, predictable or surprising, *Intent to Be* and *Sense of Being*, *I Am-ness* is present. At whatever degree it may be, the living Life unfolds.

"Whoever has ever seriously pursued science, can only be convinced that a spirit manifests in the laws of the universe, a spirit that is immensely superior to the one of man." [lvi]

And when we act within the flow of life, when the proper intent meets the adequate people, means, time and places, everything suddenly goes very fast. Life takes over and spring blossoms everywhere, even in winter. Intentions, occasions, opportunities perfectly coincide, everything aligns. The universe becomes incredibly fertile, and we are submersed by synchronicities. Just like a surfer who impeccably takes the wave, we feel the circumstances sustain and push us forward, up to the very end of a perfect trajectory. And we just want to start again, and again. And again.

And making this happen is NOT about willpower but about something else.

Willpower is a wall, not a step. [lvii]

Put your intelligence, your heart and your mind at the service of That which is within you. Let yourself be transparent in your acts, feel the moment and the energy that come from within. Let your intent come from the highest *I Am-ness* possible and discover that you stand at the core of life, like a tool at the service of a superior intelligence. Serve instead of wanting to perform, achieve or become, instead of *serving yourself*. Then you will see hardship and obstacles vanish.

Letting go is standing at the heart of the instant and feeling perfectly comfortable there. Being precisely in the moment, without wanting anything. Without fear nor desire for nothing. Just like when you walk: to dare taking a step that comes from nowhere, and another and another. To be made to walk instead of willing so. To let yourself be made to move, love and act. To be made to live.

A sort of unwavering contentment that is stable and dynamic all the same.

In this very instant, you may feel the infinite that lays behind as well as the infinite that lays ahead. A brief, derisory but tremendous sense of being. You stand at a point in time and space.

A silence.

A silence that is still, vertical and vertiginous. There is nothing but this stillness, this so minute equilibrium.

All is. Now.

Nothing is to be found anywhere but now. This is a prodigious Reality.

Our intellect is far too slow, far too narrow to be able to grasp the vastness of an instant. The only possibility, a huge one though, is merely to be aware of it and not put the intellect into play.

There, immensity takes us and shakes us like the wind a plum tree, till all fruits have fallen.

There surrender nests.

These things pass through you in a flash of awakening and only leave a vague memory *"did I really feel this? What was that again?"*
An unmanifested presence. The scent of the fragrance of perfume.
Something has passed and left a faint trace, not even a memory.

Nothing remains.

A star you are looking at, which gives you a wink. All your life, you will doubt you really saw this.

Experience all that and remain in silence.

I Am-ness

The latihan of Susila Budhi Dharma

When you are not encumbered with thoughts and emotions, when you are free from your mental bustles, all the concerns that fill your being hour after hour, year after year, when you let silence rise within (without willing not to think though), then you may be given a sensation, an imperceptible vibration which gently (or sometimes strongly) comes forth.

A presence to yourself which you never experienced before.

As if your usual sense of being had briefly changed nature, replaced by something else, of another nature that lays deep in your innermost, all at once alive, active and at peace.
A sensation that nests in you, unlocalised.
You gradually become aware, more than ever, of a life that inhabits you, a content that is suddenly clear and serene, all concerns and thoughts evaporated.

Something grows and traverses you, enlivens you, which you cannot but listen to, observe, feel, express, fully conscious of the experience. A subtle and real *presence*, that is impossible to recognize until you have experienced it.

This experience which any of us may access, is the *latihan kejiwaan* of *Susila Budhi Dharma*[1], or Subud.

Latihan means training[2]. In this context, a training to the *Susila Budhi Dharma* state, a state that opens to the *Rohani* being that is dormant in every of us: By this exercise, the entry to the deepest *presence* within us opens by itself[3]. We just do nothing, touched by a vibrant Life Force that gradually uncovers the being we genuinely are and the *presence* degree we belong to. We surrender to it, and we merge.

---

[1] *Susila Budhi Dharma* are Sanskrit terms that may translate into *the noble attitude of total surrender to Divine power,* which describes the state of a genuine human being.

[2] *Latihan kejiwaan* may translate into *spiritual training* (or training of the inner/spiritual being).

[3] This is the reason why the first time one practices this exercise is called *the opening*.

Now, truly, you put your fingers into the socket.

What you are in reality, progressively shakes you, gradually overwhelms you and you get wrung out, rinsed, inhabited with a feeling of newness which is you beyond anything you know of yourself. A *presence*. Your *presence*.

Presence.
Nothing less.

This is what the *latihan* is about: a *presence* within you, that is immensely tranquil and vast, that does not come from any exercise of mind or willpower, a **promise that is already fulfilled.** That has been fulfilled from all times.

This awareness vibration takes you as you are, where you are, in such an ordinary, almost paltry way, that the experience is somehow disconcerting at first: During the exercise, songs, movements, dances, tears, laughter, murmurs, screams or silence come to you. Sometimes a deep and authentic feeling of worship, untainted by any creed. All these manifestations are yours but do not come from the self you think you know, and which you practice daily.

For a rather short time (less than half an hour, most of the time), your whole being is in labour while the heart and intellect are at rest, you are a conscious witness of that which inhabits you, precedes you, enfolds you. An **active *presence***, that is both inside and outside you.

In between exercises, the real work begins: to live your life while trying to experience this new *presence*, to let it come out in the lengthy labour of extracting yourself from your ego, through whatever events and circumstances that may come to you. Labour as in the maieutic sense of it: bringing your real "*I*" into the world, into your very ordinary lives.

And in this, you experience humanity, majestic, trying and mundane all at once. Life as a teaching and an apprenticeship.

How does this training operate?

It literally puts your ego on pause, this story you tell about yourself, all that jams your *presence*. You gradually experience a direct link, without hindrance nor filter, with the *Rohani* being that you are[1].

Remember the previous chapters, how the sub-human *presence* fields occupy your ego and clutter you up. You know now that *wanting to* get away with them is impossible: they are part of you, they fill your ego and inner being as you constantly use them and interact with them in in all your life experiences. The only way to get this sorted out for good is to confide in That which all those forces owe their existence to, and which traverses them all. Only That can put each of these fields in order in you, hence at their real place.

Thus, the *latihan* ultimately is a training to letting go, to surrendering to the power of the Source in us, **to be channels**, nothing more and nothing less.

A prodigious support in our apprenticeship.

This vibration is a contact with the Great Life Force, that stems from the primeval *Intent to Be*[2]. It connects you to the full Reality of what Creation is.

---

[1] Cf. page 150

[2] Which is named the Holy Spirit by Christians, Roh al Qudus or Light of Muhammad by Muslims, Ruach Ha' Kodesh in Judaism.

In that respect, the *latihan* of *Susila Budhi Dharma* is an **experience of Real Life**. An opening to the *Presence* within you which is not your ego.

A junction is gradually made between the *Jasmani* and *Rohani* awareness degrees, as nothing prevents or hinders it. The door opens in you to the complete human being in this world, what is precisely and beautifully expressed by *Susila Budhi Dharma*.

Susila Budhi Dharma tells the **channel being**, the one who lets the divine *Presence* within him/her flow totally free, without any ego interference. A *presence* that is active in all the meanings of it, which radiates benevolence, goodness, care, protection and attention to all in every circumstance, in full symbiosis with the order and rhythm of Creation. A being who rejoices in the act, with no interest or desire whatsoever for any subject nor object, with no *I, you, he, she, they*, (only *us* maybe?).

A miracle maker.

A being who lives for and by something other than self. A being in love. Because Reality is only That.

A being **in** the world but not **of** this world as we are used to living it, at ease with matter but not materialistic, enjoying the company of vegetables and animals, tending to them, without being subjugated to addictions, ambitions, fears, envies and passions. A being of responsibility, free from the delusions and artifices of power.

A being who contributes to making this world a **humanity**, the manifestation of Reality and not the messy projection of our desires, of our egotistic drives, of our individual or collective separateness, where our sufferings and all that we inflict to ourselves and others, come from.

Susila Budhi Dharma is the experience of a genuine and complete human being in this world.

It is about practicing patience, surrender, sincerity and letting go while being fully active and alive in this world.

In Christianity, this experience would be described as *Revelation* or *Oratio, Haqiqah*[1] in Islam: a direct

---

[1] The first step on a spiritual path could be described as *Lectio* for Christians, *Shariah* for Muslims. It is the strict observance of principles, rituals and « commandments ». The second would be *Meditatio* for Christians and *Tariqah* for Muslims: it is about studying, searching, going deep into the texts and teachings. Then comes *Oratio* or *Haqiqah*, what here is

285

contact with the expression of the Source, without resorting to the intellect nor to the heart.

Then, very gradually, the complete, immense and profound meaning of our purpose appears. The reason for the human being to be in the world: to be a realities maker and benefactor by proxy.

Gratitude arises by itself, constant and overwhelming at the same time, for this opportunity once again given to any of us, created beings, to participate in Creation, to bear witness

---

about. Beyond, the ultimate stage of clarification would be *Contemplatio* for Christians and *Marifah* for Muslims. Similar stages may be found in Judaism: *Nefesh,* the observation of physical facts characterized by action, *Ruach,* the heart and intellect focused on contemplation so as to arouse love and awe, *Neshama,* spontaneous understanding that generates these emotions (the Kabbalah's "rapture of the heart"), *Chaya,* knowing/communing, totally in love with the Divine, with complete annihilation of ego. Ultimately comes *Yechida,* the perfect reflection of the *Ohr Ein Sof,* the world of *Adam Kadmon,* the soul as an active witness, totally merged within the all-loving endless and limitless manifestations of the Source.

https://www.chabad.org/kabbalah/article_cdo/aid/380651/jewish/Neshamah-Levels-of-Soul-Consciousness.htm of its limitless perfection and mind-boggling beauty, in the vast variety of its awareness degrees.

The time has come to **truly experience Reality**. It is no longer about making theories, predications, conferences, parables, books or talks. Or worse about experiencing our figments of Reality (have we not had enough of this?). The time has come to live it. To experience oneness with That which Is and to put an end to separateness.

In the *latihan,* we start it all over again. Everything in us is revisited because, until now, what we acted from was our ego, our creeds and all the *presence* planes that contribute to the persons we have made of ourselves.

Although we learnt how to walk long ago, we are made to walk again. Our hands, arms are moved without any intention nor willpower, our legs are moved, our voices are awakened. Although we have always been talking, we are taught again how to speak, make sounds, melodies and chants. Every gesture whether from our hands, legs, arms or feet, are revisited. In order to teach us again how to be **that which we are in Reality**, beyond what we believe we are. Then the emotions are touched, and we rediscover our laughter, our cries, our joy. Then on, our thoughts and intentions get clarified as our awareness, our *presence* degree expands. Sometimes we know, in a flash of an instant. A quiet evidence we do not necessarily feel like sharing.

Every possible way of thinking, feeling, behaving is relearnt, lived anew, this time moved by the power of the *One-Awareness* within us, beyond our will or desires. A *full reset*, being again apprentices of who we are, complete at last and opened to experiencing Reality in this world.

All along this training, we are given the possibility to feel a profound and serene completeness, as if everything was explained and at its place, while what is not has no importance whatsoever. A real state of *wellbeing*, of being fulfilled emerges. Chimeras, worries, envies are like a heavy traffic in the distance of a quiet home, where we are at peace, immersed in an immutable tranquillity.

Of course, all these things take their course back and rush in once the exercise is finished, but their grip, their weight, their importance lessen with time.

Unnoticeably, irrevocably your life changes direction, just like a train is diverted by an invisible switch. Propositions after propositions, it takes a different turn, another course. You are caught in the flow of Life, so much so that you may surprise yourself at it. Because Life is movement.

It is important to acknowledge however that you will not be spared any of the life's hassles, none. You may possibly go through impossible or even painful stuffs and realise in retrospect, after having gone through all sorts of ordeals and torments, that it miraculously ended well.

Of course, the *latihan* of *Susila Budhi Dharma* is open to anyone, disregarding of religions[1], social status, gender, age[2], cultures or nationalities. What is recommended, but this is not mandatory, is to be openly aware of the Creator reality (or possibility), therefrom the path will unfold by itself. It knows no master nor guru. The only guide resides at the deepest of your inner being, a new understanding of who you are. As such it is neither a ritual, nor a teaching nor a religion. It is no initiation, asceticism, self-discipline nor meditation. Nor is it about learning stillness, void, silence and detachment from the world. Quite the opposite rather. It changes us into **reality makers.**

---

[1] Which does not prevent from having one. On the contrary, it opens to a new and deeper understanding of it.

[2] It is necessary to be of legal age to participate .

As its purpose is experiencing Reality, our own is full of life, movements, sensations, sounds and gestures. So that we may fully manifest our human *presence* degree.

Each of us lives it at his/her own rhythm, according to his or her nature and being. This path fits so finely to everyone's nature that you feel nothing foreign, you recognize yourself in it, as a state that you have always known. Where the *latihan* takes you is who you truly are and no one else, hence this feeling of gratitude you may experience.

It is so natural that one does not need to look for it. It comes and appears by itself, when the *presence* state of the person matches[1].

Always **clarification** happens with meticulous and considerate care and respect for whom you are. There resides the absolute trust, the real surrender to What *Is*. This clarification is gradual and goes in stages:
- At first, *movements* come, which manifest Life within you as well as the clearing of the influences of matter.

---

[1] It does not need any kind of proselytising either.

- Then on, while movements develop, *sensations* come in: you rediscover touching, seeing, hearing. You smell fragrances and perfumes that come from nowhere. You see things that others do not. You feel new sensations of depth, you lose the feeling of separateness. You clear from the vegetable influences.
- Then the *feelings* are touched: cold, powerful emotions rise, which you bear witness of. You take yourself to truly love the world and the people, without purpose or cause, to share each other's emotions. You laugh or cry with no reason, you feel sad next to someone afflicted, jubilant next to (or thinking of) someone joyful, anxious next to someone in anguish, hence witnessing humanity's oneness. This manifests the clearing of the animal influences.
- Eventually, *understanding* comes, you know without having searched or learned. You act and get involved in circumstances when the need arises. Nothing more. In this state, there are no longer prayers, neither hope nor expectation. There is **active presence** and if, from there, requests spontaneously arise, you *know* they will be answered.

The whole meaning and purpose of the *latihan* is more about what we do with it than what happens in the exercise room. How we live it through our intentions, thoughts and deeds.

This exercise that is practiced twice or three times a week, on your own or with others, men and women each on their sides[1], is not an end. Rather the opposite. It is a training (an indoor training as a manner of speaking) to a state to be close to in your daily life, while acting in this world.

When you practise it in a group, you may experience the very peculiar oneness one can feel between those who share it. You touch on the Creation's oneness, what we are, while each in his/her unicity. This dual sensation of oneness and unicity is very real, deep and soothing, felt by everyone.

When you receive the "contact" for the first time, it is the whole of your being which, unbeknownst,

---

[1] While the *latihan* enables us to access and reveal our original nature where we experience oneness, it is necessary to allow femininity as well as masculinity to express in full respect and no hindrance nor interaction between genders.

becomes accessible to your human consciousness: in Reality, all is instantaneously accessed, nothing is restrained. *But* you will only very progressively *realise* it: this Reality will gradually infuse within you, as your being is being prepared and your consciousness opens. This ongoing process is gradual and continuously in balance between where you stand and what is accessible to you. It spans over years and years according to each one's nature. We leave behind one moult after the other, sometimes merry ones, sometimes remnants of ordeals, a whole path in awareness, which is precisely what being human in this world is about.

The Marvel among marvels unveils very gradually. It adapts very finely and precisely to where you stand on your path, and needless to say that it does not depend on your will, wishes nor envies.

The *One-Presence* is only love and respect for each one of us as well as all that is created, to a point we have no idea.

Then on, all comes to you at your very own measure, **in a perfect and constant equilibrium between the inner and outer**. Wishing to hasten the process would only be an interference of the ego, which has nothing to do in this passage. What you become "in awareness" manifests through

new circumstances that come to you, novel life
propositions which, in their turn, raise another
awareness and, in this way, the path moves on.
What you are and what you believe is revisited
again and again and again and again in an endless
evolutionary spiral.

Hence, all is gradually **clarified.**
Our whole being is infused by the *Clarifier*.

Idhafi.

The inconceivable Life Force that spans across the
whole universe.

We are traversed by the life vibration, *Idhafi*,
begotten by the divine Essence, wherefrom come
our most exact inspirations, our most fertile
thoughts, our most selfless acts. Our most real joy.
We are fully immersed in *Qudus,* the infinite divine
Awareness, wherefrom come our deepest sense of
being. Our most real contentment.

We have a taste, at minute doses, of the reality of
What is.
Precisely there, you comprehend, in the form of
your own words and truth, all what has been
described above.

The other reason for these movements, these chants, is that every part of your body, each cell is touched by the Great Life Force. All your senses, your perception capacities are worked upon. They are purified at first, then prepared, transformed and ultimately revealed to themselves.

Hence, your whole inner being is taking shape with **functions** which become truly its own, unfettered from the lower forces' influence. This is the **resurrection of the senses** (and not of the flesh) as evoked in certain religions.

I pity those who say there is no resurrection.
The flesh does not resurrect,
But what is it that can resurrect,
So that we can revere it?
The Breath (pneuma) animates the flesh (sarx).
There is also this light in the flesh: the Logos.
...
You must awaken while in this body, for everything exists in it.
Resurrect in this life. [lviii]

It is our functions that live again and are integrated in the beyond, not the body that is made of flesh and bones, all organic matter, which is only of this world. Our functions are awakened, accomplished because they are freed from the imprint of the lower forces. The human being is complete not only because it realises the dual union (between manifested and non-manifested worlds, between masculine and feminine) but also because all its functions are activated in Reality.

Hence, the *latihan* of *Susila Budhi Dharma* purifies, prepares, reveals the sight and the capacity of seeing, the hearing and the ability to hear, the smell and the ability to smell, the taste and the ability to know flavours, the touch and the capacity of apprehending, our capacity to feel, our thought-consciousness. You may perceive things that usually are inaccessible. For example, you may feel from the distance the thoughts, pains and joys of someone you feel close to.

Here your spiritual body takes shape, what you are in the here-after. Here all is in its place.
Here you access one the deepest purposes of this training: to retrieve your being integrity, including and mainly in the here-after, to become a complete human being, in its senses and purpose. You access the Kingdom.

Here ends your apprenticeship.

I Am-ness

AN END WITHOUT A STORY

We knew it before the start: words are outperformed, too slow, too short, too numerous, too minute for what they convey and contain.

For the immeasurable power of That.

The voyage that finishes here never stops; it is an end in itself. A book with no other story than yours.

The one that was told at the beginning is not a story. It was the mere description, certainly unperfect and lacking, of **an unthinkable flash.**

After all this journey we have travelled in awareness, you may have let It penetrate and inspire you. From now on, it will come along with you, enabling you to live anew within it.

Now, here, any time you wish, as often as possible.

At the end of this journey together, remember one thing: **What you know is only as worthy as what you do with it.** Hence this little book will have no other reality than what you make out of it, the intentions that will get born from it.

What matters is in the act, the verb.
This is the human reason for being.

Through the act, you complete your apprenticeship.
Through the act, you manifest "*I love*" at its very best.

Telling one's love to Life, to the Origin is a strange experience. The heart is at loss, rattled by the proximity of the ultimate Gigantic. How can the flea whisper its love to the elephant that carries it? It can only let itself be transported in awe and confidence to where it goes, while it wanders, hops and gets lost on his back.
Then, through the act simpleness, one learns how to be satisfied with the tiny, which is not insignificant.

All what we came to live has just to be lived. All of it. Whatever the choices we make. Each step towards Compostela must be taken, none can be avoided, but once taken, none has to be made any longer.

All that happens to us does come in due time, at the precise right moment. Nothing happens by chance, nothing we can avoid. All our decisions, choices, hesitations lead us to the very same place whatever it is: to precisely live what we came here to live. There can only be one single destination: the primeval Reality that inhabits us.

Where we come from is where we go.
This is the Path towards Oneself.
And it winds through the improbable meanders of our intentions, our projects, our emotions, fears and joys. All that makes a life.

Everyone can only live, comprehend, become aware of what one must live, comprehend, become aware of. All must be re-dis-covered, it is as simple as that.

The Source touches you and smiles to you, constantly.

By the delicate crumpling of the flower, the clouds running away, the busy flight of the bumblebee, the joyful trills of the lark, the glittering shimmers of the sea, the weaving meanders of the desert dunes. The song of the world.

The rain that crackles and the thunder that rumbles.
The children that play too and the crowd that rushes out of the underground.
And that look, beautiful or in askance, you caught.

Stop as often as possible and marvel at it.

All these words, all that noise you have read and shared, have at the end of the day one single reason for being: to bring you at the threshold of your own path towards silence.

Because the signal is silence.
.

I Am-ness

APPENDIXES

The discovery of the latihan: the opening

This is no ceremony nor ritual. Just the first exercise, the first *latihan,* nothing more. Those who participate in it have been practising it for long enough to be able to receive the vibration in its integrity, hence making sure that the newcomer's experience will be as complete as possible.

Would they be in their own agitation, it would act as a filter which would reduce the experience's reality. Just like at a concert, if everyone is coughing, sniffing or fidgeting, you cannot hear what you came to hear.

One starts the exercise with a moment of quiet, everyone turned inwardly, quietening his/her thoughts. All are sitting relaxed in silence, attention inwards.

Then the newcomer simply tells her intention, the intention of her being there, why she wishes to engage in the *latihan*. The intention ought to be sincere[1], expressed loudly and directed to the highest possible, to the Source, God, Allah, Havayé, the creative Origin of the universe. Or simply the possibility of a Creator. It is important to express that one confides the whole of one's being, that one surrenders the whole of one's existence to the Source, without fear, without restrain and with sincerity and trust. Some use the word worship, why not, this is a beautiful word if it tells a truth that is profound and lived. If it tells a creed, something learnt, a ritual or a reality outside of oneself, one had better choose another word that would fully be one's own. Words are of little importance, what matters is their content, the intention, and to express it.[2]

Then, those who share the exercise with the newcomer advise to relax, peacefully and to

---

[1] If you seized the importance of intention in the Reality of what Is, you may understand that sincerity is here neither a rule nor a constraint, just the condition for the experience to really unfold.

[2] For the newcomer's intention to be resolute and fully informed, a three-months waiting period is usual before the first *latihan*. Hence, the path unfolds within before it manifests in the outer.

trustfully surrender to whatever comes, to put aside any desire, fear and thought. They ask him or her to close his/her eyes and pay no attention to whatever happens around him/her, to those who practise the exercise. Lastly, they recommend not to be afraid of unvoluntary movements, chants or sounds that may arise.

In order to begin the *latihan*, there is no need for formulas, rituals or any address. The simple words *"relax, receive (or begin)"* suffice. They tell the trust in the Life Force one surrenders to.

Then the exercise begins, each one letting oneself go. This is as simple as that. Each time, it is an experience that is proper, specific, different. It can be very gentle, profound or powerful. Or sometimes nothing specific. Or disconcerting sounds or gestures. As long as it lasts, it suffices to be attentive to the feelings that arise, to the origin of the sounds and movements. One focuses one's consciousness onto what happens to oneself, even if this is silence or nothing. One does not preoccupy oneself about what is around, about the sounds one may hear. One lets the others where they are and worry about nothing. The *latihan* time does its work, whatever shape it takes. Whether the sounds are heard or not, whether they or the movements are harmonious or not is of no importance whatsoever. They express a work that begins.

There are no two identical *latihans.* Each participant expresses his/her own and, more importantly, it changes with time, as and when all the parts of the being are touched.
At some point, the vibration or feeling fades away and the exercise spontaneously comes to its end. All remain in peace and quiet, attentive to what has just been felt and received. Then it will probably be the proper time for a good coffee or tea, to get to know each other more closely.

Here is something that is no detail: what is received only belongs to you and you cannot be called for an account of it or talk about it, if you do not wish to. Only willingly may you talk of what you have lived. **All that matters is that you do not try to understand.** Do not allow the intellect, apprehensions, curiosity or willpower to take hold of what does not belong to them. Let the exercise make its way within, at its own pace; each of us is accountable for himself or herself of what he or she does with it. It may be useful however, especially at the beginning, to tell experienced others about questions, doubts or fears even which you may have, to prevent the heart and mind from getting in the way. Similarly, the helpers who will have shared your first *latihans,* may enquire if you felt anything: it is essential that the experience gets real from the start, that something is perceived.

It is critical to realise that nothing in this exercise happens, that would come from outside of oneself. This is a profound and intense relationship between I and *I.* Therefore, there is no reason whatsoever to fear anything as nothing foreign happens. And if tears or even pain happen, just let them go, this is something that is detaching and finds its way out.

Many are those who surprise at the simplicity of the moment. Most of the time, one is touched by a feeling of peace, of deep serenity, of bliss or grace.

This opening is a reality, this contact feels real, a real that is beyond you, enfolds you, nourishes you.
That loves and respects you.

After the opening

From then on, it is rather simple. Each one lives his or her life in a normal way. Each has his friends, her job, his family, her relationships. Daily lives unfold with all what they call for and bring forth. Henceforth, one discovers that one has two guides on one's path: the *latihan* as a bi-weekly training and *life* itself, which reveals it is endowed with intelligence as it naturally passes on messages and proposals.

Gradually everything takes a new flavour, as if one had been given a sixth sense, something that adds to the experience of being alive. Everything takes on a particular colour, whether it be happiness or sorrow, effort, aches and joys, work and rest.

You live, while trying as much as possible to be aware, not to reload yourself with what is being clarified. This is not done through burdensome and enclosing discipline, but simply through a particular attention to the choice you make. You try as much as possible to make them in full awareness, and if a silent voice whispers *"are you sure?"*, to listen to it if you can.

Once on this path, one should walk it, keep this little flame alive, with patience, regularity and trust. Practicing the *latihan* twice or three times a week is recommended, but one has to keep within the flow of life: do not force things if life circumstances do not allow such a frequency, but at the same time, do not give way to procrastination, to the small temptations which, for one reason or another, suggest postponing this date with oneself.

Do not want to overdo it either (the key word here is "want"). There will be weeks with three *latihans*, others with one, say twice is an average.

A small piece of advice: it is better not to drink alcohol at least six hours before practising the *latihan:* alcohols (*spirits!*) are subtle and very powerful vegetal essences and these can quite unnoticeably hinder or veil one's receiving, deviate it even to the point of being a source of confusion.

Then on, life follows its course with its meanders, highs and lows. Transformation is rather gradual. Habits or preferences spontaneously change, they go by themselves, nearly unnoticeably, something like belongings one gets rid of while on the way, when one realises that the backpack is too heavy.

The tests

After having practised the *latihan* for a while, it is possible to get, through it, answers to existential questions or about one's inner development.

This practice, called *test,* makes it possible to receive through the body, through movements or feelings, an answer to a question that is asked preliminarily to the exercise. In that instance, the exercise is rather brief, one minute or so, the time for penetrating oneself with the feeling and its nuances. It is recommended to do *tests* sparsely, prudently and precisely. It is essential to do them with several people, with helpers and members having an extended experience of the *latihan.* Too many interferences (heart, intellect, likes and dislikes, a priori and preconceived ideas, deep and diverse influences) may get in the way and meddle with how the answer is perceived. The questions must be articulated with care by *helpers,* free from any personal interest or opinion about the matter. It is preferable to do the *test* in a quiet and peaceful environment, far from the daily hubbub. It is ideally done after a *latihan* which results in uniting the inner beings of the people who share the *test*.

Putting together the feelings that have been received, which may be different, makes it possible for a multifaceted response to emerge, which ought to be pondered upon. Life is complex and any question has implications at various levels which colour the answer. If the expressed feelings diverge far too much, it is likely the question was not properly asked or inadequate. In this instance, a peaceful and unbiased conversation with the concerned person usually allows the subject to be outlined and clarified before starting again.

This process is not about crafting a majority: All perceptions are to be considered even if, in the end, it is up to the person at the origin of the question to form his or her own opinion based on his or her own feelings.

Testing is a precious tool and gift, which requires practice and experience. It may be tempting, especially in the beginning, to misuse it and resort to it even for everyday or personal decisions. In this case, one will quickly experience how inappropriate this is, especially through the confusing and disconcerting, if not catastrophic, results one will draw from it. It must be clear that the *tests* are intended to measure out and support the evolution of one's inner being, to understand one's attitudes towards life and its trials, or to discern how the *latihan* is working within. They cannot replace the normal use of our intellectual, relational and emotional faculties in life and the responsibilities that are ours.

Subud

Subud is the name of the community of those who practice the *latihan* of *Susila Budhi Dharma* [lix]. This community counts some twelve thousand members worldwide, of all religions, countries, cultures or social backgrounds. This number is relatively even over the years, between new entrants and those who, for one reason or another, stop practicing.

The founder of Subud is an Indonesian, named Y.M. Muhammad Subuh Sumohadiwidjojo (1901-1987), respectfully named Bapak[1] by the members.

---

[1] Pak or Bapak is a mark of respect which means Sir or Father in Indonesian.

He was the first to receive the contact, in a very unexpected manner, when he was twenty-four. The experience has regularly kept on and grown for many years, during which he was given profound and repeated spiritual experiences which brought the process to its end. The awareness rapidly came to him to pass on the *latihan* which then spread all over Indonesia and around. Bapak was invited in Great Britain in 1957 and from there the development of Subud as an international organisation began. However, as he himself stated, *"Subud is not foreign. It belongs to no country, just as it belongs to no race or creed. It did not 'originate' in the East, and it did not 'come' to the West. It comes from the Spirit of God, which is nowhere a stranger."*

The organisation (a non-for-profit association) likens somehow exactly the *latihan* process which is both an inner transformation and its expression in the world. Hence, the Subud reality is of two facets that are different but constantly work together:

- A spiritual side: *helpers* who are members with a long time *latihan* experience, oversee the *openings and tests,* tend to the *latihans* and the possible needs for clarification from members. Becoming a helper comes with a particular process at the end of which the capacity of the candidate is confirmed by a *test*. The helper's role is permanent, but it is possible to withdraw for a while, for personal or practical reasons or because the person takes on organisational duties in the organisation.

- A material side: the organisation in charge of making the practice of the *latihan* possible in the most appropriate conditions, mainly by acquiring and managing halls that are dedicated to the exercise, as well as funding for material contingencies (travels, publications, meetings, archives…). Financial contributions to the organisation are totally free (one obviously accesses the *latihan* disregarding of resources conditions). For its financial needs, the organisation receives the support of the Muhammad Subuh Foundation (MSF), a foundation which handles the funds collected for Subud.

This two-sided organisation goes upwards: it starts from the local level ("groups" organised with local helpers and committee) upwards: regional, countrywide, zonal (the 9 major regions of the world) and worldwide.

The life of the brotherhood and the direction it wishes to take, are collected during World Congresses (an AGM that take place every four years, each time in a different country). The Congress (whether world or national) is the only decision-making body for the organisation. Hence, the Subud nature is made of its members who decide upon its orientation and not some directors or committee of experts.

In between World Congresses, an executive office implements the Congress decisions, while the whole community is represented by a Council made of representatives of each zone (the world regions) as well as international *helpers*[1].

In this way, the life and needs from local groups are carried forward at the regional, national, zonal and worldwide levels, which secures that the organisation truly represents the brotherhood

---

[1] In the same way, there is an intermediary body at the zonal level: a council established upon the same model with a zone representative supported by country delegates for the organisational side and helpers (one man, one woman), for the spiritual side. This reproduces at the country level, with a national council made of group representatives as well as national helpers.

reality. This organisation makes it possible to share good practices on the material level and makes sure that the *latihan* is practised along the lines that were transmitted by Bapak. Mandates are generally on a four-year term which cannot be renewed, which makes it possible to rotate the various roles among members.

Practising the *latihan* naturally prompts the being to develop and express in various arenas according to each one's nature. Hence, the Subud association has initiated affiliate organisations (the "wings") which support developments in various activities, be they charitable, cultural, in the field of health, education or business, each similarly organised at the international, national and even local levels.

*   *   *

I Am-ness

AFTERWORD

What this book tells, results from the experience of someone who has been practising the latihan for nearly forty years and let his life be driven and changed accordingly. It expresses neither a dogma nor truth and certainly none that would be declared or claimed by Subud, which declares or claims none.

What is described here is told under the unique responsibility of its interpreter and he surely has, more than once, messed up with the Reality he endeavoured to tell. He will gladly welcome any comment that would let him know.

May every reader forgive him for anything in these pages that may be inaccurate, offensive or out of place. Nevertheless, how imperfect it is, those who are on their Way or practise the latihan will undoubtedly find echoes and similarities with their own experience.

I Am-ness

Table of Content

I Am-ness 3

FOREWORD 5

PREAMBLE.. 11

Ultreia! 13

The story begins................................. 15

THE INTENT TO BE 43

A path.. 45

Where do we go?................................ 45

How do you know you are on the right path?
.... 55

Alive! 58

The *Presence* fields of Creation 63

The first *presence* degree: the material nature
.... 70

The second *presence* degree: the vegetal nature 84

The third *presence* degree: the animal nature
.... 97

What can we do with these subhuman awareness degrees? 108

The fourth *presence* degree: the manifested human nature 124

The fifth *presence* degree: the real human nature 150

The sixth *presence* degree: the nature of Gift 158

The seventh presence degree: The nature of Love 162

The Marvel of marvels 167

Our five powers.............. 173

The power of love 180

The power of *presence*............ 188

The power of intent, the content (*Dhat*) .. 196

The power of form (*Sifat*)............ 199

The power of resolution (*Asma*) 202

Thus, the act is born............ 207

Our vehicles................ 225

Our thought form: The ego 225

Our physical form: the body 246

EXPERIENCING LETTING GO 259

Life is alive!................ 261

The latihan of Susila Budhi Dharma 279

AN END WITHOUT A STORY 299

APPENDIXES 305

The discovery of the latihan: the opening 305

After the opening...................................... 310

The tests.. 312

Subud 314

AFTERWORD 321

NOTES 326

NOTES

i Dao De Jing (I)

ii *Higher, farther!* Joyfull greeting of the Compostella Pilgrims.

iii Leibnitz

iv Dao De Jing (I)

v Cf. the Christ letters

vi Talking with Angels

vii The Christ letters

viii Talking with Angels

ix The *Roh Raewani* nature (Islam)

x The Gospel of Mary Magdalena p8 1-8.

xi Under the influence of the *amarah* force (Islam)

xii The *Roh Nabati* nature (Islam)

xiii Cf « the secret life of trees » (Peter Wholleben)

xiv Under the influence of the *aluamah* force (Islam)

xv The *Roh Hewani* nature (Islam)

xvi From Susila Budhi Dharma (Bapak Muhammad Subuh Sumohadiwidjojo)

xvii Under the influence of the *supiah* force (Islam)

xviii The Gospel according to Philip plate 108-40 (J.Y Leloup)

xix The Christ letters

[xx] The *Roh Jasmani* nature (Islam)

[xxi] The Gospel according to Philip plate 112-60

[xxii] Genesis 1 (26-27)

[xxiii] The *mutmainah* force (Islam)

[xxiv] The Christ letters

[xxv] The Christ letters

[xxvi] The Gospel according to Philip (plate 117- 71)

[xxvii] Etymology: Mutual dependence relationship between people.

[xxviii] The *Roh Rohani* nature (Islam) -

[xxix] The Gospel according to Philip (plate 109-44)

[xxx] The Gospel of Mary Magdalena p8 19-24

[xxxi] The Christ letters

[xxxii] The *Roh Rahmani* nature

[xxxiii] In the Hadiths of Islam, *Ar Rahman* is one of Allah's names, which means "the Compassionate, the Merciful"

[xxxiv] The *Roh Rabbani* nature (Islam) – the *Atziluth* world (Judaism).

[xxxv] Rabia, a Sufi mystic of the 9th century.

[xxxvi] The Christ letters

[xxxvii] The Christ letters

[xxxviii] Talking with Angels

[xxxix] Dao De Jing (LXVII).

[xl] The Christ letters

[xli] Talking with Angels

[xlii] The Christ letters

[xliii] The Christ letters

[xliv] Dao De Jing (III)

[xlv] Talking with Angels

[xlvi] Wei Wu Wei (Terence Gray) in *Fingers pointed towards the moon.*

[xlvii] John 14 :10

[xlviii] The Christ letters

[xlix] The Christ letters.

[l] Hui Hai (Wei Wu Wei op.cit.)

[li] Anand Merothra (This is That)

[lii] Wei Wu Wei (op.cit.)

[liii] Wei Wu Wei (Op.cit.)

[liv]. Dao De Jing VII

[lv] The Gospel according to Philip P70 p116

[lvi] A. Einstein

[lvii] Talking with Angels

[lviii] The Gospel according to Philip Pl.105– 'If someone has not first resurrected, they can only die' (Pl. 104- 21)

[lix] Subud is the acronym of *Susila Budhi Dharma*

Printed and bound by CPI Group (UK) Ltd, Croydon, CR0 4YY

25/09/2024

01037886-0003